MW00611960

Opening page artwork:

Insomnia stalked me during chemotherapy. My pattern was to awaken at three or four in the morning after a fitful sleep. I would pour a cup of coffee, pray (simply) and write in my journal. This first drawing is a picture of the view from my living room chair at sunrise. Just as the sun rose every single morning, I prayed that I would also rise.

FEELING THE SHIFT

Cancer, Faith, and Kindergarten Art

Pat Clark

www.revpatclark.com

AUTHOR'S NOTE

The essays in this book were written during a two-year period beginning from the time I was diagnosed with stage 4 cancer in September 2015, until I started treatment for its relapse two years later. Most of these essays began as posts on the website www.CaringBridge.com where I documented my journey. Initially, I wrote for my children, extended family, and friends, to keep them informed about my treatment. Then it morphed into wanting my kids to have a legacy about their mother and her faith.

To my surprise, many people enjoyed reading my blog. They asked permission to distribute some of my posts to their friends. Others encouraged me to compile them into a book that could be helpful to people who were undergoing cancer treatment or other traumas. Half of the people who read my blog were churchgoers. The others would never set foot inside the walls of a church.

Some of the things I wrote were raw as I tried to stay afloat emotionally during this period. Looking back, I don't remember the discomfort. What I remember is how much love and kindness I received. I have a brown paper grocery bag full of cards people sent and a 17-page list of gifts people mailed or brought over to the house. My family rallied around me in remarkable ways. All of that kept my spirits up and enabled me to endure. I am grateful to be on the other side of treatment, grateful to be alive, and grateful that I feel well. I regret never writing thank-you notes. In large part, this book is a thank you to all of those who prayed for me, commented on the Caring-Bridge site, came for visits, and sent food, cards, and gifts.

The experience of surviving stage 4 cancer has birthed an unexpected new career for me as a writer. This is my first book. I hope there will be others. For my readers, let me say at the outset: Whatever hard thing you are facing, you can overcome it. This book will show you how I did it, and hopefully, these techniques will work for you.

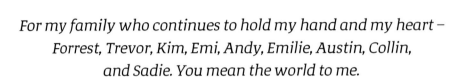

For my family who continues to hold my hand and my heart –
Forrest, Trevor, Kim, Emi, Andy, Emilie, Austin, Collin,
and Sadie. You mean the world to me.

CHAPTERS

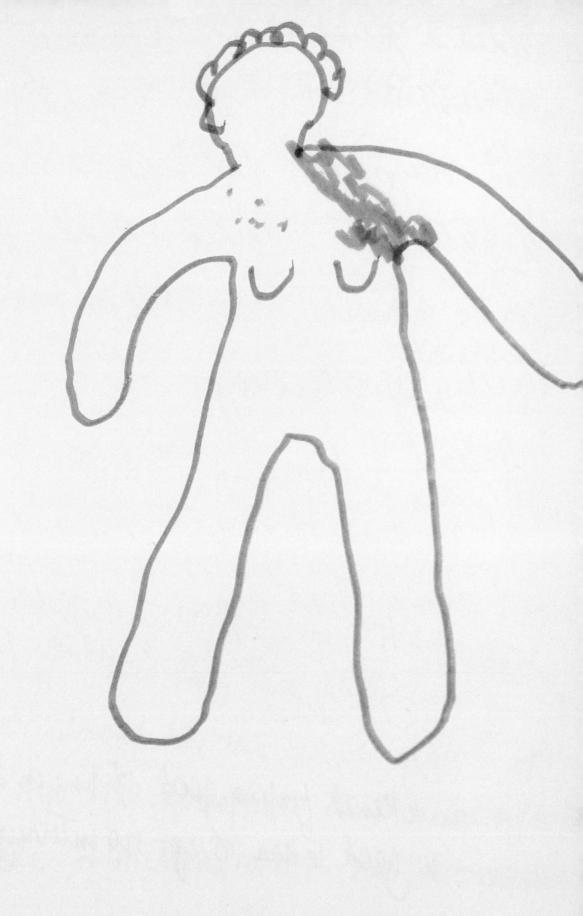

BEGINNING

Fear not, for I have redeemed you. (Isaiah 43:1)

*I*t was Rosh Hashana, September 15, 2015, the day Jews believe that God opens the book of life and decides who will live another year. Dr. Francesco Turturro, an Italian born oncologist on staff at MD Anderson Houston, came in, shook hands with my husband Forrest and me, and seated himself at the Formica-topped desk in the small examining room. Speaking with a gentle Italian accent, he told me, "You have follicular lymphoma. It's normally slow growing, but this one has turned aggressive, and we need to treat it right away. You will have very strong chemotherapy, six doses, one every three weeks. Your hair will fall out after the first treatment. You may lose all feeling in your hands and feet, and that could be permanent. You will have cramping and constipation or diarrhea. You must gargle water with baking soda constantly to prevent mouth sores from forming." He droned on, but I did not hear anything else he said. I was on over-whelm, shut down mentally and emotionally. It was all white noise at that point.

I went numb on the inside, which is my usual method of coping with stress. I felt nothing. Zero. I noticed how small the room was, how ugly it was with its antiseptic-looking white walls and gray furniture. I saw the fresh white paper pulled over the examining table. In my mind, I focused on everything else in that room except his voice. I wondered why they were keeping what looked like large plastic urinals in one corner.

My annual checkup with my primary care physician only a month before had been stellar. Yeah, I had lost some weight, but that was a good thing for someone as hefty as me. I had bruises, but I have always had bruises because of low blood platelets. I was tired, but I have been tired my whole life.

On that day, my doctor had pronounced me healthier than I had been in years.

As Dr. Turturro spoke to me about my diagnosis in matter-of-fact tones, I thought back to the day only a month before, August 14, 2015, the day of my last mammogram and sonogram. The radiologist himself had exclaimed, "Wow! Would you look at this? This is not anywhere near a normal cell! Wow! It's all the way above your clavicle bone! Your breast is full of it!" There was a pause while he repositioned me to look at the other breast. "Look, there are abnormal cells all over the place on this side! I hate to be the bearer of bad news, ma'am, but I think I am looking at cancer here. You need a biopsy right away."

I was stunned that day. Tears filled my eyes. The assistant gently helped me off the gurney. "Take care of yourself, ma'am," she said tenderly. I stumbled to my car and drove home. There I told my husband, and we agreed that if it was cancer and I underwent treatment, I would be treated at MD Anderson. He was stoic, as he usually is, but he held me close.

During the week that followed, I was like a little wounded, whimpering bird. I cried off and on and felt sorry for myself. Nothing can prepare one for the time when a doctor says, "You have cancer." I think it is always a shock—at least it was for me since I was essentially symptom-free. The whole world changed right then and there. If you don't know what is important in your life, those words will flush it out. Immediately. My first thought? "I can't die! I haven't traveled enough!" I wanted my family close—my husband, children, and grandchildren. I wanted them gathered around me and huddled together, like circling the wagons.

I scaled back everything and told only a few people. My family came first, and they were terrific. My daughter is the pastor in the family. She very gently probed how I was doing and how I was reacting and feeling. She expressed concern without sharing her feelings. She said, "I want to be there for your chemotherapy treatments." The thought comforted me. My son came over to the house. We didn't talk about feelings, we never do, but there were tears in his eyes as I told him everything I remembered the doctor saying. "You are strong," he said, "and have overcome many hurdles. You will overcome this one too." He gave me a big hug before he left.

I also told the two small groups I am a part of—my colleague group of women ministers and our movie group. A half dozen or so of my clergywomen friends had come for lunch one day. We were snacking on strawberries when the telephone interrupted us. I answered it, and a kind woman from MD Anderson told me the results of my recent CT scan. "There is a large mass in your stomach area in addition to your breasts and clavicle area, and we are referring you to the lymphoma clinic." "OK," I said. She continued, "You will have to have several biopsies so that we can be 100 percent sure, but we are 98 percent sure this is lymphoma. They will contact you soon." She was clinical and matter-of-fact, and so was I, on the outside anyway.

I tried to take it all in as the group chattered on. I told them, "That call was from Anderson. My stomach is full of cancer. It's everywhere. They are referring me to the lymphoma clinic." My friends all seemed as shocked as I was. Kathleen said, "Now? You learned that information just now?" "Now," I told her. "That was the telephone call I took." "Oh, my God!" someone said. "Oh no!" someone else said. "I am so sorry," was the response from yet another. They all had a look of deep concern on their faces. I was still reeling.

One of the ministers blurted out, "My ex-husband texted me on the way over here that he is getting married." "What?" we all shrieked. "Pat has cancer, and he's getting married again so soon?" "Yes," she said and started to tear up. Lynn said, "I think we need some wine. I have some in my car. Let me go get it." Without waiting for an answer, she left, went outside, then quietly returned with a bottle of Chardonnay. I set out wine glasses. She opened the wine and poured us each a glass. We began to laugh then. Everything—cancer, ex-husbands, problems in church—it all became hysterically funny. We laughed and laughed as tears streamed down our faces, and we had a wonderful time! It was perfect, the perfect medicine after a cancer call, a profound emotional release for all of us. The laughter helped everyone feel better. We bonded as a colleague group that day.

The next week I was admitted to MD Anderson's lymphoma clinic, and over a two-week period, I had blood work, an EKG, a CT scan, a PET scan, biopsies of my breast and stomach, and a consultation. Sydney, the farm dog, seemed puzzled having to wake up to go outside when she was used to sleeping in and not getting her morning walk. She would leap to greet us when we returned from my many appointments, and that cheered us both.

I had wondered whether I would even accept treatment. I was feeling fine. If I accepted treatment, with all the side effects Dr. Turturro mentioned, I would never again feel as good as I did then. My immune system was already weak. It would become even weaker during chemotherapy. Traveling posed a great risk. A simple infection could be life-threatening. I was sad and disappointed that I would be housebound for months. I worried about pain and nausea and vomiting. What if the treatment did not work, and I had to go through all the side effects anyway? In my mind, I saw a big question mark where my future was concerned.

As a pastor, I had known many people with cancer and had watched some of them thrive while others died. I had seen the nausea, the neuropathy, the life-time wearing of sleeves to prevent swelling, the exhaustion and the depression. I wondered if I could go through all of that—mentally, emotionally, and spiritually. Was I strong enough to endure? What impact would chemotherapy have on my body, my mind, and my spirit?

I had a sense of completion about my life and was not afraid to die. After all, by this point, I had more loved ones on the other side than I have here on Earth. I felt sad, though, when I thought of leaving my husband, Forrest. I met him when I was 17 years old, and we have been together ever since. He is my one great love, and the thought of being anywhere for long without him upset me greatly. The physical act of dying didn't bother me but letting go of loved ones would be difficult. It's hard for me to let go of clutter, much less treasured relationships. That was the toughest part to think about. I cried every time I thought about leaving Forrest, my children, and grandchildren.

I have journaled for most of my life and used that to process feelings. I wondered about the deeper issues that were undergirding this lymphoma. Now, on August 23, I drummed up the courage to take out my journal and have a conversation with my body as art therapist Lucia Capacchione had taught me. Years before I happened onto her book, *Recovery of the Inner*

Child, and it became life-giving to me. Lucia teaches that the nondominant hand accesses the right brain, the deepest part of oneself where one's inner wisdom is located. One writes specific questions in longhand with the dominant hand, switches the pen, and answers the query with the nondominant hand. The results can be surprising. I was so mesmerized by her work that I trained with her and became certified in her method of art therapy, Creative Journal Expressive Arts. For years this work kept me afloat in dealing with troublesome feelings and people. It gave me a safe and gentle way to process whatever was happening in my life by drawing my feelings onto the page, then journaling with them.

Lucia healed herself from a serious health condition years ago by doing this kind of journaling. It set her on a path to become an art therapist, helping thousands of people deal with traumas of every kind. Now I would put that work to the test as I never had before.

As she had taught me, I began to write to the crude purple image on the paper, alternating between my dominant and nondominant hand. The dominant hand asked the questions; the nondominant hand, that accesses the deepest part of oneself, answered the questions. This is the simplest method I know for accessing my inner wisdom.

With my right hand, I asked my drawing, "How do you feel?"

My left hand answered immediately, *I am suffering. I have no filters because I don't have good boundaries.*

With my dominant hand, I continued with question No. 2, "How can I help you? What do you need from me?" She replied through my other hand, *Listen to me and do what I tell you. Quit taking cues from everybody else. This did not happen overnight. This is a lifetime issue—trying to please everyone and do what they want. This truly will be a journey into darkness, but don't be afraid. The cancer won't kill you. You have many years to live.*

In that instance, I felt goosebumps. I knew the voice was speaking the truth. I had always been motivated by what needed to be done and focused on meeting others' expectations, even if I was sacrificing myself in the process.

Lucia's method of journaling with the nondominant hand has often shown me the deeper issues underway when I have had unwanted emotions like fear, sadness, and anger. Most often I use four questions: Who are you? How do you feel? What is your message to me? What do you need from me? This time I only used two. I could tell by the shift within my body that I was right on. I knew it deep within me. It's hard to describe the inner feeling of truth. I just knew it. I also knew this work would be foundational in getting me through the cancer experience.

Cancer has lots of causes. I know that. We live in a poisonous, stressful world, practice poor lifestyle habits, and eat chemically laced food. I have come to believe there is a strong emotional component to cancer, and the body is indeed a great teacher. I have spent most of my life avoiding conflict and caring more about others' opinions than I do mine. Frankly, I have never figured out what the origin of the inner voice is—whether it is my true self, the Spirit of God, Christ within me, or what. I know only that I can usually access it quickly through the nondominant hand, and that process will cause my spirit to come back into balance. Serenity means everything to me these days, and I will seek peace over anxiety any day of the week.

Shortly after the dialogue with my drawing, the Louis Armstrong song, "What a Wonderful World," began to play over and over in my head:

> *I see trees of green,*
>
> *red roses too*
>
> *I see them bloom for me and you,*
>
> *And I think to myself what a wonderful world.*

Gradually, hearing it within me for so many days, it began to speak to me, not only of gratitude but of cherishing the life I have, every part of it, even this troublesome part that involves a life-threatening disease.

I am a Christian. I believe that God communicates with us in many and varied ways. Now I believed that God was telling me there were lessons unfolding through this situation that I needed to learn. For months before my diagnosis,

I had a deepening sense that God was preparing me for a new calling. I had been thinking the new calling would reveal itself as a minister to a church somewhere. Boy, was I ever wrong! This new call of mine was nothing less than an invitation to go through cancer and its treatment, experiencing God in the midst of it. Could I learn to trust? That seemed to me the central issue.

I was grateful to be at MD Anderson. The buildings there deliberately engage the right brain through beautiful sculptures, aquariums, and pictures everywhere. For me, they became places and ways to experience and reflect upon the divine. For instance, lying on a gurney for what seemed like hours awaiting my breast biopsy on the first day of September, I noticed a lovely picture of a rosebud, hanging on the wall, all pink and tightly closed before its moment of gently unfolding. Immediately I felt an instant kinship since my middle name is Rose and since I was in the beginning of my cancer journey just as the rose was beginning to unfold on hers. I asked what she had to tell me, and this emerged through my nondominant hand: *All is well, Patty, and all manner of things will be well. You will come through this smelling like a rose. There is a sweet part to all of this, and beauty and simplicity will prevail. Look for the visuals as you walk this path. That fabric dragon you saw when you walked in the door represents your inner strength. You are tough enough to do this, and you will do it with joy and a sense of humor. Don't be afraid. See me when the going gets rough. You will be a tree of life.*

Now I admit that I am sometimes skeptical of what the nondominant hand reveals. There are times I think it is just my giving myself a pep talk or surrendering to grandiosity. I could be saying what I want to hear. Who knows? I thought of the Virgin Mary when the sky filled with angels, and shepherds showed up to see her baby, Jesus. Scripture says, "...Mary treasured all these things and pondered them in her heart" (Luke 2:19). I too pondered these things I was receiving through the nondominant hand. I looked for confirmation from other sources like science and medical tests, friends, family, and Scripture. I wondered. This was just the front end. Would it hold true in the end?

Lying on that hospital gurney, I decided to take it one day at a time. I believed there would be a sign of grace every day that I endured. I could not say that I would enjoy the year, but I knew that I did not walk alone because Forrest was with me, and I felt the presence of God was also with me. That brought me enormous comfort.

WEDDING VOWS

In one fell swoop, on September 14, my oncologist, Dr. Turturro, canceled all my magnificent plans. I bargained, "Can I go to Puerto Rico and the Virgin Islands? I already have tickets!"

"No. There's no hospital on a cruise ship."

"New Orleans? We have a wonderful trip planned with friends. We have reservations!"

"Too risky. You could get an infection. An infection could kill you right now. You must cancel everything. You cannot be around crowds of people during treatment."

"I cannot cancel the wedding in Austin this weekend. I have known Andrew since the day he was born. I've spent too much time with him and his fiancée, Meghan. I must officiate that wedding! I have to!"

"OK," he said cautiously, treading lightly on my feistiness. "We will do the bone marrow biopsies on Friday, and you will start chemotherapy on Monday." Both events were less than a week away.

Forrest and I drove to Austin that Friday. My fatigue was worsening, and my body was growing stiff. Suddenly my health issues felt real. I had two big gauze patches on my hips where techs had taken biopsies and given me instructions not to bathe for 48 hours. Loopy from the sedation, I could barely sit up in the car. Not only that, the puncture wounds still hurt. There were sharp pains in the muscles surrounding both hip bones. I could not get comfortable no matter how I sat. I was grateful Forrest was driving. No way could I have done that. I was nervous about sounding coherent that night for the rehearsal. I prayed the bandages wouldn't show through my clothing. *Help me not to embarrass myself!* I pleaded. *I don't want anything going on within me to distract from this couple and their ceremony.*

I was frustrated that I had been diagnosed with stage 4 cancer without either showing significant signs of the disease or feeling bad. In fact, I had prayed that God would give me some symptoms of the disease, so I could feel better about undergoing chemotherapy. After all, why go through this massive, severe treatment if I felt just fine? God answered that prayer in a matter of days. The lymphoma began to assert itself.

I was exhausted. Not only that, once an hour, every hour, I began to "glisten." Moisture trickled down the back of my neck. My hair became sopping wet where it touched my neck. Beads of sweat broke out on my forehead and trickled down my face. My legs stiffened like boards. I could barely go up and down stairs because they had lost so much flexibility. I remained determined. Nothing would stop me from the wedding.

The wedding would be held in the chapel of the Presbyterian seminary in Austin, Texas. It's a replica of the one John Calvin had built in Geneva, Switzerland, where Presbyterians trace their roots. I had a lot of memories from there from when I was in seminary. Andrew's parents had married in that chapel many years before. That explained why we were returning to the seminary campus. Also, Meghan had graduated from the University of Texas across the street. The rehearsal was like herding cats, full of young people having a wonderful time. We finished and headed for a magical Mexican dinner on Town Lake.

The day of the wedding I sat in a room off to the side of the chancel awaiting the ceremony. One of the musicians asked me what my favorite Scripture was. "These days," I told him, "it's the words of Jesus on the cross: *Into your hands I commit my Spirit.* I don't have any control anymore. This cancer has the upper hand. Right now, it seems to be controlling me, but ultimately God is the one in control. I can only surrender to that." The music started. We were about to begin.

One by one the 10 bridesmaids strolled down the aisle as the groom, his groomsmen, and I awaited them in the front of the chapel. The bridesmaids wore pastel shades of gray, lavender, and blue, all of them different. They were gorgeous! Then I felt it—the glisten. I hoped no one noticed. Finally, the bride appeared in all her glory, and oh, she was beautiful! Andrew stood resplendent in his tuxedo. We were all filled with emotion. Beads of sweat ran down the sides of my forehead and moistened the hair on the side of my head. I acted as if all was perfectly normal.

Andrew choked up when it came time to say his marriage vows, repeating them to Meghan as I whispered, "I, Andrew, take you, Meghan to be my wife." "I Andrew, take you, Meghan, to be my wife." I continued. "And I promise before God and these witnesses to be your loving and faithful husband." Back and forth, we continued, "In plenty and in want, in joy and sorrow, in sickness and in health." Then he repeated my words and enthusiastically and joyfully provided his own ending, "...forever and ever and ever and ever!!" She repeated the vows with her own tears and the same ending, they exchanged rings, they braided a cord to illustrate their Scripture passage from Ecclesiastes, we prayed, and voila! I pronounced them husband and wife. They left with much joy and fanfare through a shower of confetti and headed to their reception at a place out of town. I smiled at them and glistened, sweat pouring off my brow.

I thought about the vows of the young people as Forrest bagged up my clerical robe and took it to the car parked outside the chapel. He was taking care of me in my season of sickness as he promised in a similar ceremony 50 years before in a Methodist chapel only a few blocks from where we stood. We had repeated the same vows to one another in another ceremony full of emotion. I did not know or understand much about God then, but there was a presence or holiness in the little chapel on that afternoon. It was serious and wonderful and brimming with love. After our ceremony, we were as excited as Meghan and Andrew. I remembered a photo in our wedding album where we wore gigantic smiles. We were thrilled that afternoon finally to be married.

Now 50 years later, with me in sickness, Forrest was still honoring his vows. He had taken off work and gone to every medical appointment with me at MD Anderson, and they were legion. His was the first face I saw when all the scans and biopsies were completed, and I often staggered out, weak and disoriented. He planned for, shopped for and cooked many meals, then washed the dishes afterward. He ran every errand to drug stores, grocery stores, pet stores, and everywhere else. He continued to do all the laundry, a pattern he began more than 40 years ago.

He held me when the tears flowed and let me cry the sadness all out. Forrest cried only one time that I remember. When we sat with an insurance clerk the first time I went to MD Anderson, his eyes watered, and a few tears escaped down his cheeks.

He made sure that I was comfortable by bringing me pillows and throws wherever I was planted and adjusted the temperature of the house. He made sure there were plugs and cords nearby for my electronic devices.

Forrest took it all in stride. He helped me up and down difficult-to-navigate stairs and in and out of cars, usually sitting me on a nearby bench while he brought the car around. He did all the driving. He pretty much did everything. A lot of people offered to help. Forrest would not let them. I was his mission those days, his grand project, and he did all his caretaking without complaint.

I made it through dinner at the wedding reception, but the glistening and the fatigue worsened. We left the wedding before the first dance and drove back to Houston. More and more sweat was pouring off my body.

One never knows the impact of decisions made early in life, how they chart our course. I never imagined growing old. I certainly never considered having cancer. People in my family generally drop dead of heart attacks. It's all over in a flash. My father, mother, and only sibling died in their early 40s. I never expected to live past 45 years of age.

I don't think I understood our wedding vows then as a young bride madly in love. I had no idea what it would mean to live them out. The front end of a marriage is all about hope and possibility and merrily facing challenges hand in hand, or it was for me anyway. I could never have predicted the "in sickness and in health" part. I was barely 20 years old when we married. I could not think past the imminent future of the Vietnam War. We were safe, or so I thought, because we were married.

I remain grateful that Forrest took his vows seriously that warm and sunny Tuesday afternoon in the little Methodist chapel. How different this cancer experience would have been without that! I have always believed that God sent him to me, and I am immensely grateful. I am grateful also for his huge servant's heart that knows no limits. I do not know what I would do without him. The impact of this nasty disease would be far worse without Forrest.

He is the finest example of faithful love that I have ever known.

Like Meghan and Andrew, I get choked up when I think of how my husband has lived his vows to me for 50–plus years. I felt again like Mary, the mother of Jesus, who said in a very different circumstance, "I am blessed among women." We were filled with the romance of the wedding as we drove back to Houston, even as the sweat poured off me.

CHEMOTHERAPY, DAY ONE

September 22, 2015, was an incredibly bad, horrible, dreadful day.

Forrest and I showed up at MD Anderson to get my PICC line installed. The PICC line (I have no idea what the initials stand for) is a semi-permanent, intravenous port used for giving chemotherapy. The line goes into major blood vessels in the body since the smaller veins in one's hand or arms could collapse or "fry" under chemotherapy. Watching the video about precautions and maintenance in a small room off the reception area was more than I could bear; I began to weep softly. I cried for the sadness of this period of my life and for my feeling like a doofus for walking around with stage 4 cancer and not even realizing that this nasty lymphoma was stealthily taking over my body. I mean, who does that? Who wouldn't know? Am I that completely and totally unaware of my physical self? I felt ashamed and embarrassed.

A clerk ushered me into a room with a gurney where two Filipino nurses were waiting. The young male nurse noticed the silent tears leaking from my eyes. As I lay on that sterile, skinny gurney, my body covered with a cotton hospital gown, he began to sing in an effort to cheer me. "Come on," he said, "Dean Martin—you know," and then he began to sing, *Everybody loves somebody sometime; everybody falls in love somehow....*

"Do you like that one? Do you remember? How about this? *When the moon hits your eye like a big pizza pie, that's amore..."*

I tried to sing with him through my tears, my voice cracking all over the place, while the other nurse repeatedly stuck me with a needle: *Volare, oh-oh,* "Ouch!!" *Cantare, oh, oh, oh, oh, oh...*"AHGGGHHHH, that hurts!!!" *Let's climb way up to the clouds.* I tensed up like a board. Inside my vein, the needle was stabbing—prick, prick, prick! She was torturing me, or so it felt. Apparently, my vein grows smaller as it heads upwards to the upper arm. They were going through my arm with that PICC instead of my chest because my chest was full of tumors. The male nurse kept singing, trying to distract me from the discomfort of the repeated stabs.

Finally, the sweet syrup they had given me to relax began to kick in, and I started feeling woozy and unconcerned about the pricks. God only knows why they did not wait for that to happen before they began all the stabbing. The drugs helped greatly, but what helped even more was when another technician, who entered the room with a smaller needle, efficiently and effortlessly inserted the PICC line. I was done! Because of the medication, I was groggy and disoriented and forced to stay at MD Anderson until noon when its effects would wear off. I could barely sit up! My head rested on my chest like the elderly people one sees in the halls of skilled nursing facilities.

A precious friend whose job it is to escort Very Important People around the halls of MD Anderson unexpectedly showed up to see me. Immediately, I became her very important person. She took one look at me and asked, "Do you need to rest?" I nodded my head. "I thought so," she said, then took me to a hidden, quiet room off the beaten path at MD Anderson. It was darkened and filled with couches and recliner chairs. She pointed to an empty couch. I lay down, and a volunteer handed us a warm cotton blanket and pillow. Forrest covered me with that glorious warm blanket. I felt enveloped in the warm and loving embrace of God. I rested, and the experience was pure grace. There I was, laid out like a corpse in the middle of the day in that bustling hospital in a darkened, silent room. It was heavenly! It wasn't completely quiet, though. A man on a nearby couch snored so loudly that sleep was impossible. I did not care; I was too wiped out.

A couple of hours later I had more blood tests, then a visit with my doctor and his assistant, Ly who told me, "The tests show that your heart is strong. You should be able to tolerate chemotherapy just fine. The bone marrow biopsies of your hips came back. You have lymphoma in 40 percent of your bone marrow. They both showed the same amount."

"Oh, that's bad!" I blurted. "No, actually," she said, "that's considered moderate." I interpreted this as good news. "You're good to go," she told me. "We have scheduled you for chemotherapy at four o'clock."

"What??" I gasped. "I can't! I am exhausted! I am already worn out from that dreadful PICC line experience!"

"Well," she told me emphatically, "we won't be able to get you in this week if you don't do it today. Look at it this way. You're already having a bad day; why not just get all the bad over with and have a better day tomorrow?" "OK," I said reluctantly, but my heart wasn't in it. Forrest and I left the clinic and rode the elevators down to the second floor.

I did not feel strong enough. I did not know how I would ever make it through. I was worn out and tired, feeling like a lamb led to the slaughter. In my mind's eye, I saw Christ hanging on the cross, willingly choosing to die when he could have avoided it. Here I was in what felt like a similar situation. I do not know that I have ever dreaded anything more. No, I didn't sweat blood like he did, but I prayed with him, "Lord, into your hands I commit my spirit." It was a bad day, and it got even worse. So much for answered prayer, I thought. Now it seemed like everything depended upon me to get through whatever followed, and I surely did not feel up to the task.

Downstairs, I climbed onto a hospital bed and watched as the nurse brought in an armful of bagged drugs, $50,000 worth, most of them clear liquids, except for one that was bright red. I have never learned to pronounce the names of any of them, but I know the red one they call the red devil. It's the one that makes your hair fall out, gives you nausea, and a whole host of other unpleasantness. The nurse hung the bags on a metal tree beside my bed, then hooked the first of the clear ones to my PICC line. The slow drip started going into my veins. It was painless. I was grateful. So far so good. She left the room. Forrest left to move his car to a different parking garage because the garage we had parked in earlier would close before I finished chemo that evening.

I began to shiver. Minutes later a friend entered my room, but not just any friend. Susie is a no-nonsense, don't mess with me, military general type of nurse who has treated cancer patients for years. As we talked, I shivered more. I felt freezing cold, and my body began vibrating! Susie swung into action, moving quickly into the hall and yelling for a nurse. "Nurse!" she ordered. "Get in here! Now! Right now! Right here in this room! She's having a reaction!" I was shaking so hard that I worried I would vibrate right off the bed. My blood pressure spiked. The nurse came quickly, stopped the drip, and gave me a shot of Demoral®. I began to vomit, again and then again and again. Susie repeatedly emptied the basin. Under normal circumstances, I might have been horrified. On this day I felt too sick and nauseous to care.

They waited an hour until the vomiting stopped and my blood pressure stabilized. They resumed the vein drip, but at a much slower pace. Once things were under control, Susie left, and Forrest returned. I did not vomit again, nor was there any pain, but it was difficult to stay in an uncomfortable bed for the 12-hour experience. Several times I got up and walked around, dragging my tree full of dripping bags as I walked. Silently, silently, the wondrous drugs were given.

The slower pace meant that Forrest and I were unable to leave the hospital until 4 in the morning. We practically limped to the car, both of us worn out. I felt over-medicated and drained but grateful that I was not also recovering from surgery. I had no pain anywhere in my body. I have never been happier to see my dog and my own bed.

Things did not turn out as I had planned that day. It was a difficult, hard experience. So often people go through things, and it all turns out hunky dory and beautiful, and they say, "God was with us! God is good!" OK, I get that.

But what about me? Did God abandon me on my initial voyage through chemotherapy and leave me hanging to fend for myself while God was busy working miracles somewhere else? Once I might have believed that, but not anymore. I think God is good whether we have a fabulous experience or we land in a dark hole somewhere. The clearest theological statement that I can think of is simply this: Shit happens. We do not live in a perfect world. Terrible things happen to all of us. Newscaster Robin Roberts quoted her mother saying, "Everybody's got something." It's true. We all must suffer at some point in life. How we endure forms our character for the good or for the bad.

The clearest example of God's grace during my night from hell with chemo-therapy is that I was able to endure. I went through the experience, and I walked out on my own two feet. It ended. It did not last forever. My overwhelming feeling was gratitude that it was over.

Like Jesus on the cross, I could say, "It is finished."

SIGNS OF GRACE

Years ago, our family had a cat named Snowball, a beautiful, fluffy white cat that we dearly loved. We let her have far too many litters of kittens before we had her fixed because we loved having fun and playful kitties around, they were always gorgeous, and we were able to give them away easily. Whenever It was time for Snowball to give birth, she would lead me to her chosen birthing room, most often Forrest's darkened closet that smelled of leather. I would sit with her for several hours of hard labor, stroke her fur, and give her loving words of encouragement as she pushed her babies out.

Years passed, and it came time for her to die. She was gaunt and haggard-looking, and then she stopped eating. I was heartbroken! As she prepared to leave us, she again wanted me beside her as she began the process of active dying. I sat for several days and nights with Snowball, thanking her for a wonderful life of service to us, telling her how much we loved her, stroking her fur, and giving her permission to let go. She neither ate nor drank and could no longer walk. Forrest finally took her to the vet, who put her down and ended the terrible suffering. I was devastated. Anyone who has loved a pet understands.

The next week, I had an appointment with my perky spiritual director, and we walked together into a comfortable sitting room with soft couches and chairs at the Cenacle Retreat Center in west Houston. She closed the door, and I told her, "My cat died last week, and I am still a little teary."

"Where was God when your cat died?" she asked.

"Nowhere!" I said emphatically. "God is never around when you need him!" I felt resentment when I said it, as though I had been abandoned.

"God was there," she told me. "You just didn't see. Here's your homework: Ask God where he was and come back next month and tell me."

I left the quiet and peaceful surroundings of the Cenacle with its tall, noble pine trees and kind, gentle people, then steered my car out into the noisy and chaotic Houston traffic with roadblocks and construction workers. Proceeding down Memorial Drive, I gripped the steering wheel and prayed, "So, where the hell were you?" The answer floated into my consciousness as clear as a bell and revolutionized both my faith and my theology. The inner voice said, softly and gently, "I was the cat."

Spirituality moved into my gut that day. As a longtime Christian, I have always believed in the Trinity and the essential tenets of the faith. I still do. Here is the shift. I thought God was out there somewhere in the heavens, but God was also among us, especially in Scripture, praise, and worship. God was also within me in my devotional life. Suddenly I saw that grace surrounds me; that God comes to me each day in a myriad of ways that I ignore mostly or fail to label correctly.

The day after chemo, sipping my morning coffee from the ugly chair in the living room, I relived those moments with Snowball. I wondered about the signs of grace that may have been there in my day of miserable chemo. The day my precious cat died, I sat there stroking her and speaking softly. She looked at me, and with no words, just the look in her eyes, I felt profound love. I felt appreciated for the care I had given her and was giving her in that moment. I felt her gratitude. I do not think that I have ever experienced as deep a sense of connection before or since as I did in her dying and looking at me with those eyes of love. It was beautiful and bonding, and now it would change my life to realize that God was with me, had always been with me, even in the darkness. It took a suffering and dying cat to open my eyes to the deep truth that God is with us whether we perceive God's presence or not. I thought of the powerful love Snowball and I had shared in her final days and was overwhelmed with the love of God. Even though her death was more than 20 years ago, the experience left a wonderful memory.

I tend to spend my life on autopilot, going through my day and checking off items on my to-do list, then collapsing into the bed at night. I am usually much too tired for reflection or to notice the signs of God that appear. The horrible first day of chemotherapy was no different. It was a bad, terrible day, and I had no feeling of the powerful love of God. So where was God in all the unpleasantness of my 20-hour passage through hell, other than in my endurance?

The next morning I retraced my steps through that day, asking God to show me where he/she was. This is what I discovered. As I started with the early morning PICC line experience, I remembered a child's drawing of an angel lying on a table outside the room where I was to have my vein stabbed. Primitive and childlike, it was sketched on a white piece of paper and left on a coffee table. When I thought of it the morning after, it was as though God was speaking to me through that child's artwork: "You are indeed surrounded by angels as you go through this."

Then there was the kind nurse who sang Dean Martin songs to me as the other nurse repeatedly jabbed me trying to slide in the PICC line. I love music—especially the songs I grew up with. I could still hear him singing, and it made me smile. Although uncomfortable, no permanent damage was done. His happiness reminds me of the Scripture: *...the joy of the Lord is your strength* (Nehemiah 8:10).

When I look back on the day, I don't think about the discomfort; I remember one lovely voice singing to me: *Volare, oh, oh, Cantare, oh, oh, oh, oh. Let's fly way up to the clouds, away from the maddening crowds.*

Perhaps it was an invitation to place my thoughts on higher things.

There was the Quiet Room at MD Anderson, a darkened space filled with couches and recliners hidden away, a place few patients know about. Kind volunteers bring you pillows and cover you with warm blankets. I was able to rest for a few hours before I began my first chemo. Reliving the experience, I heard the words of Jesus, *Come to me, all you who are burdened and heavy laden, and I will give you rest.* I could not have imagined such a gracious place of rest to prepare me for the next worst thing I would experience.

There was Elizabeth, my angel and friend, who works at MD Anderson and knew all about the Quiet Room. Without her, I would never have known about the room, but then there is this—the timing of her appearance that day! At just the right moment she showed up and facilitated my rest. Was that just a coincidence? I don't think so.

Reliving my day, I remembered Susie, veteran cancer nurse with 20 years' experience at MD Anderson. She showed up during my chemo and witnessed my violent reaction, vomiting and shaking so terribly that I practically leapt off the bed. She saw my blood pressure spiking. She emptied my vomit basin and put cool towels on my forehead. Her presence alone calmed me and perhaps saved my life. Coincidence? I think not.

There was also a sweet, young volunteer pushing a cart through the halls during that long horrible night. She carried an assortment of soft knitted caps that church ladies had knitted and supplied for cancer patients at MD Anderson. I tried on several of them, checking myself in her hand mirror until we both decided on the one that looked the best for me. She was pure grace. I later wore that multi-colored cap nearly every day. It felt soft on my bald head.

There was Sydney, the farm dog turned city girl, who greeted us when we came home, wagging her stump of a tail. Dogs have always reminded me of God because of their unconditional love. Sydney, a sweet Australian Shepherd, licked my hand when we came home and would later become my constant, daily companion.

And then there is Forrest, always Forrest, with me for the entire 20 hours, sitting in an uncomfortable chair, providing steady comfort and loving support, never complaining, always strong.

So yes, God is with me, even through the suffering, and I give thanks. Slowing way down (and I was becoming more used to living slow), I had more time for reflection. How many things I have missed in my life by failing to notice!

I remember the teachings of St. Ignatius of Loyola who urged people to reflect on their day each evening, by remembering the places that brought them joy and happiness and those that took happiness away. Too often I focus on all the negative things without remembering the good and lovely things that have been a part of my day. I vowed to be more intentional in doing this simple exercise.

KINDERGARTEN ART

The Lord is my light and my salvation; whom shall I fear? The Lord is the stronghold of my life; of whom shall I be afraid? (Psalm 27:1)

An e-mail changed the entire cancer experience for me. An artist friend now living in California wrote that Psalm 27 had come to her when she was praying for me that morning. She felt compelled to share it.

I had read the Bible through several times and taught Bible study for years. The learning from that had made my passage through seminary a breeze. But on this morning in my first week of chemotherapy, the psalm startled me as if I had never seen it before: *The Lord is my light and my salvation; whom shall I fear? The Lord is the stronghold of my life; of whom shall I be afraid?*

I decided right then I would do *Lectio Divina.* This is an ancient process from the early church used to personalize Scripture. You read a verse or verses and wait for a word or phrase to "shimmer" a little or to stand out more than the others. You then meditate and pray with the word or phrase. It's a simple way to nail Scripture to one's soul. I decided to do that with Psalm 27, but words overwhelmed me. I blamed chemo for killing my concentration and focus. Chemo brain was settling in. What should I do when words fail? I thought artwork might help. Torn paper collage would be easier than writing.

I remembered a retreat I attended once in an artist's home in New Jersey. She had several pieces of art where she had glued fabric onto canvas. I thought I might try it with construction paper. I sat on my couch in the quiet morning imagining this dark world I live in with so much unrest nationally and internationally. Not only that, my life and body were in turmoil because of the lymphoma. Where would my refuge be? I immediately thought of the womb, and this phrase, *In Him we live and move and have our being.* It comes from the book of Acts (17:28) when the Apostle Paul addresses the Athenians. When in life do we find ourselves completely surrounded by anything other than when we are in the womb? In my mind's eye, I saw a tiny infant, held securely within her mother's womb. Of course. That was the image I had to create right then. I went searching around the house for art materials.

The word "stronghold" popped out after I read the first verse. Instantly I knew that was my word. Reading the notes on the bottom of the page in my Bible, I discovered the word "stronghold" had an alternate meaning: refuge. Immediately, the word "refuge" took hold in my spirit. It was like a magnet attaching itself to my heart.

I have never been an artist. I don't know how to draw anything—literally. My artistic skills stopped developing after I marched out of pre-school at 4 years of age because a teacher criticized my choice of colors for an art project. A spiritual director first taught me about expressive arts, and Lucia built on that, changing my life in the process. Expressive arts show the primitive, raw part of me. I get it out on paper as best I can and sometimes dialogue with the images. The work is crude, but gentle, and if I can silence the powerful inner critic that lives within me, it becomes valuable and healing.

On this day I found some old construction paper, then tore it in pieces and glued it onto another piece of whole black construction paper to be used as a backdrop. I chose the color pink, and then tore the paper up to show myself. At once I felt all girly and frilly. I am usually not a pink person and smiled to myself as I worked. Torn red pieces of paper illustrated the cancer. It's an angry color—like war or something. I certainly felt like there must be a war going on within me. Over my body, I cut and then placed a white, three-fingered piece of paper, representing the light of God and the tree of life covering me. I imagined pure light streaming into me.

Looking at it, I could see that I was surrounded by love on all sides, held securely and protected where the loving God alone is enough, my source and my strength. My cancer-ridden body rested in God, and I was completely covered by the Triune God who would ultimately destroy this nasty disease. I decided that was my message from God for the day. God was at work in my behalf. The energy shifted within my body. It was like a turbulent sea that finally calmed down.

Doing the simple torn paper artwork that I called "kindergarten art" (because it is so easy that any child can do it) brought me to peace, and my spirit was finally able to pray: *Oh God, help me to endure this in a faithful, graceful way. Show me the lessons I must learn, my great protector and redeemer. Have mercy and allow me to reflect your love and grace. May I always trust you more than any fearful, dreadful thing that will come against me.*

The late psychiatrist Carl Jung worked in Germany with people who had been traumatized by war. They had seen loved ones die, their homes and cities destroyed, and other terrible atrocities occur. He discovered that if he could get people to draw their misfortunes onto paper and then to reflect on those drawings, they could be healed. It worked every time. The power of the visual to bring healing has been documented again and again. People who did this visual journaling did not allow their misfortunes in the war and the horrible, brutal things they endured and witnessed to define them. They were able to move deeper within themselves and move forward instead of wallowing forever in what had happened to them.

I decided Carl Jung must have been on to something. I did not know whether the process would work to bring healing in my case, but I knew that I had to try. This first exercise made me feel content and more centered. I thought of the Quakers who had taught me years ago when I first entered seminary. They had asked us to visualize strong hurricanes like we experience here on the Gulf Coast, the times when the storm brews, winds whip everything around, and giant ancient trees become uprooted. Flood waters can not only ruin homes, but also kill those who are stranded. We were used to the turmoil that ensues when the weather forecasts change to Category 3, 4, and 5 storms.

I remember one of the last big ones that blew over the Houston area. This was before Harvey. The trees began to dance and swing their arms while the winds bellowed their scary song. It was frantic, and the electricity went off and on in the house. Soon there came a calm within the storm. Everything came to peace, and this lasted for a few minutes until the strong winds started up again. They continued their destructive path as branches swayed and torrential rains dumped on rooftops.

The Quakers say that the storms of life happen all the time, but the trick to getting through them is to find the quiet eye in the center of the storm. In that eye there is perfect peace. Though hurricanes change course and move, the task is to remain centered in the eye of the storm, to move with the storm, and to stay in that inner place where the storms do not overtake us.

Cancer was the biggest storm I had faced in a decade. Could I find the center of the hurricane and stay there? The kindergarten art I did that evening helped immensely. I don't understand how ripping and shredding and laying pieces of construction paper on a page helps. I know only that the first picture I made guided me to serenity that night. I had found the eye of the hurricane. Shyly, I took a picture of my crude artwork and posted it to Facebook. I felt a little embarrassed. I mean, I have advanced degrees, and this looks like something a 4 year old would make.

It surprised me how many "likes" I received. Not only that, people responded that they loved it. Would the artwork have continued without such positive feedback? I do not know, but I felt encouraged that I may have found a process to help me through this nasty disease. It seemed to me I was indeed being held securely in the womb of God and was surrounded by love. On that night I trusted this was enough. I lay down my worries and slept well, imagining the tree of life covering my stricken body, a tranquil little baby completely at peace, and it helped. I felt a shift in my spirit from turmoil to peace.

DEALING WITH EVIL

When evildoers assail me to devour my flesh–
my adversaries and foes–they shall stumble and fall. (Psalm 27:2)

I don't want to write about this. It makes me uncomfortable. I don't like talking about war. I don't want to talk about evil and what I think about it. I don't want to mention all the things I do not know. Even though I have two degrees in theology, I really don't know much, and I hate to admit that I, The Reverend Mrs. Know-it-all, doesn't know shit when it comes to cancer. The more I learn, the more I do not know. There are great holes in my theology—places where I do not understand, places where I wonder why in the world a loving God allows people to suffer. If you look around, suffering is everywhere.

I don't know why I got cancer. I don't really know about evil. I don't know why bad things happen to good people. I don't know if anybody knows. But there was something clearly amiss in my body, and I did not know why. Why did I get cancer? Yeah, I had been sedentary my whole life. Yeah, I was over-weight. Yeah, I had lived with chronic stress all my life. I had always lived by the maxim, "Feel the fear and do it anyway." I'm a tough bird.

I understood anxiety, fearing a dreadful stepfather's rages, fearing the Vietnam War and the draft of a husband earmarked for the infantry, and fearing being left destitute under a bridge somewhere because of financial issues. Oh yeah, I knew all about stress—constant deadlines, live reports, dreadful events to witness. Then there was my whole preaching career, standing up to speak for God. That one will stress anybody, I tell you. I had walked into truly awful situations, like witnessing an execution, and then got up and went to work the next day. I did most all of it juggling family time, trying to raise two kids, and caring for my husband, but at the day's end, I lay limp on the couch. I was too exhausted even to wash my face or brush my teeth before bedtime. I was lousy at self-care. I was just trying to survive.

Somehow, during all the stress and trying to do it all, this cancer quietly and unknowingly seeped into my body. Now it had flooded me, from groin to neck. Where did it come from? It's anyone's guess. They told me not to blame myself. I did anyway. I felt guilty that I neglected myself for so many years. I never did have very good boundaries. Everything else and every other person always came before my own needs.

"Why did I get cancer?" I asked my doctor, the kind, soft-spoken Italian.

"I don't know," he said, "No one knows. There are probably lots of reasons."

I thought of conversations over the years with people whose loved ones had died suddenly. "Why did this happen?" they asked me. "Is God punishing me? Have I done something wrong?" What I always told them, and what I still believed to be true was simply this: God doesn't punish us but walks alongside us and enables us to endure.

Why do terrible things happen to people? Sometimes we are the victims of human sin, like innocent people who live in war-torn countries. Sometimes we are in the wrong place at the wrong time. We live in a fallen creation, and the truest theological statement that I can offer is what I said before: Shit happens. Theological arguments are useless in the face of suffering. All the intellectual knowledge doesn't do any good when one is living in the throes of soul-bending adversity.

I could not figure all of this out, but I began to entertain the possibility that this cancer could somehow be evil. I have always hated people who blamed the devil for everything wrong in their lives. You know them, those who see evil everywhere and are always going around "binding" Satan and yelling at him. They're in a traffic jam, and it's the devil's fault. They didn't finish their work because the devil caused so many distractions. It strikes me as a way to stay a victim.

But sometime early in this cancer experience, the thought occurred to me that evil could be at work. Frankly, I do not have much energy to run around binding Satan. I can remember Joel Osteen's mother over at Lakewood Church screaming at the devil during worship. She used to say, "I know you don't have to scream to make the devil leave, but it just feels so good to do it!" Then she would scream some more, and everyone in the crowd who was watching would holler and yell with her. That's never been my style.

I am not a fighter. I am a lover. I have no trouble apologizing to anyone for anything, even when I don't think I'm guilty. Sometimes that's the only way to move things forward—just say I'm sorry and get on with it!

But fighting cancer like a warrior? What would that look like for me? I cannot even imagine. For one thing, I was tired. Most of my life consisted of lying around a lot. I am seldom angry. I get excited when an angry thought comes into my mind. I enjoy it because it is so rare. Battling the devil? Umm, not really.

So, what should I do—just lie down and let the cancer roll over me? Whine a little, have a pity party? Stay in bewilderment wondering why it happened in the first place? All of this sounded like some variation of being stuck, really stuck. I would never figure out the why of this. I could see only one option: What do I do now that this has happened?

I brewed a cup of white tea, and I thought as best I could, not always easy when one is in the middle of overwhelm. I sat in my study in front of the lit Sacred Heart of Jesus candle and a miniature statue of an Oscar. I looked around at the books and trinkets that line the wall while I sipped my tea. I stared at the computer, and suddenly I felt it. I felt a flash of anger rise in my body-a feeling of "How dare you??!!!" It started out small, then began to grow within me, like a volcano erupting. I felt my face flush as my body filled with anger. I didn't shout. I didn't scream. I just felt the rage at that cancer, felt its power, and I said loudly and boldly in the silence: "No! You're done. You stop now."

Inside I imagined a brick wall. I had reached my tolerance level. No more little nice girl. I sat there and resisted the cancer with everything I had. It was the living picture of NO! within me. I took a stand. I talked to cancer in no uncertain terms: "You will not destroy me. Your day is done. Your time is over. From this day forward, you will retreat." I meant it with everything in me.

I don't remember ever taking a position like this with anyone or anything else. I don't like to box myself in the corner. When arguments get heated, I withdraw. I don't argue because I'm not all that good on my feet. I like to think a little before I respond. Conflict makes me nervous. I deal with it when it's small before it starts escalating. Once things get worked up, I get uncomfortable. Oh, I have thrown a few fits around my husband over the years, but he's different. He's committed to me. We used to argue all the time when we first married. Not much anymore. We mellowed, a lot. I quit trying to fix him.

I decided a little artwork would help me express myself. I found some old construction paper, then tore it in pieces and glued it on a whole piece of black construction paper to be used as a backdrop. I chose a green piece of paper, then tore it and used it to illustrate myself. Torn red pieces of paper again showed the cancer. That's the anger part too—my anger at the invasion in my body. I imagined that nasty cancer leaving my body. I sat there, watching it spill out onto a heap as I worked. Over my body, I cut and placed fingers of white paper. They are streams of light for me, and I imagined the pure light of Christ filling me and touching all the places where cancer had been, the light of God and the tree of life covering me.

Again, I began to journal: "Who are you?" I asked, and through my nondominant hand, the image responded: *I am Pat standing tall*.

I queried, "How do you feel?" The answer came quickly: *Relieved this is leaving my body*.

Putting the pen back into my dominant hand, I said, "What is your message to me?" The nondominant hand answered: *This battle is mine. All you have to do is stand in my love and light. I am healing you. Let me fight this battle*.

"What do you need from me?" *Stay grounded in my love*.

I knew, again, that God was at work on my behalf. The energy shifted within my body. Whereas before I had felt resistance and anger, now I felt completely at peace. A turbulent sea finally calmed down. Finally, I was able to pray, and I said with authority: *When evildoers assail me to devour my flesh—my adversaries and foes—they shall stumble and fall.* (Psalm 27:2)

THE VIA NEGATIVA

Though an army besiege me, my heart will not fear; though war breaks out against me, even then I will be confident. (Psalm 27:3)

For five days after chemotherapy, I was given two little pills of Prednisone®, a steroid drug that helps curb inflammation, and man-oh-man, were they ever doozies! This was the end of September 2015, the fifth day of chemo, and it was like having a Roman candle from the Fourth of July shoot through my body. Tingly flashes raced through my feet, my legs, my hands, and my head all day long. It wasn't constant. I never knew when to expect it. I guessed these might be the sensations that druggies talk about when they describe what it is like to be on speed. I was wired on that stuff—no naps and no more than a total of four hours sleep per night that first week, even with a sleeping pill. You could have called me zombie woman.

The fourth night on chemo, I slept until 6:30 in the morning, a first, but then it was 3 a.m. when I last looked at the clock. That's when I had Forrest root around for some leftover nausea meds they had given me in Chicago last year when I broke my arm. One of those under my tongue and I was out cold. Before that, my blood seemed to be running like ice in my veins, and I couldn't get warm. No number of blankets piled on top of my body could take away the chill underway within my body. Usually I would sweat. That's what lymphoma patients do. We live with permanent hot flashes, regardless of our age or sex. Most often I could never get cool enough. Things flipped around that night when I felt like I was freezing. It didn't last. Before long, I was burning up. This is a strange disease, and the treatment seemed stranger.

I lay there in the night glistening, and I thought of Holy Week and Jesus' sweating in the Garden of Gethsemane before his arrest and crucifixion. Sometimes there is no avoiding the suffering that life brings. An event shows up, quite suddenly and unexpectedly. It is unwanted and unwelcome, and we are plunged into what the ancients called the *via negativa*, the path of suffering, the path nobody in his or her right mind would ever choose. When we suffer, we are on the *via negativa*—the negative way. It forms our character. We learn things we never wanted to learn. It was too early to say what I was learning from this cancer.

I never chose it. I did not want it. I did not enjoy it. I did not like the treatment, but I would have been dead within a matter of months without it. I was not yet ready to die, and so the only road open to me was to walk this path that millions were walking and had walked before I ever came into this world. In my mind, I kept hearing the African-American spiritual play over and over in my mind: *We must walk this lonesome valley. We have to walk it by ourselves. Oh, nobody else can walk it for us. We have to walk it by ourselves. You must go and stand your trial. You have to stand it by yourself. Oh, nobody else can stand it for you. You have to stand it by yourself.*

Yep. This was my trial all right. I was doing it.

I remembered the final prayer Jesus prayed from the cross. It is the prayer everyone in Alcoholics Anonymous knows by heart in one form or another: *I am in a situation that has become unmanageable for me. I acknowledge there is a power greater than myself who can manage it. I surrender my life to that power.* This seemed to be the only prayer I could pray as I faced something so completely out of my control. The cancer and its treatment overwhelmed me. I did not think I had what it took to tackle it. I was unsure if this proposed treatment was the right one. I didn't know if my doctor was any good. I could not control it or figure it all out. I could only surrender my life and place it in God's hands, trusting that God would get me through this. I was not a Roman Catholic, but the image of Jesus, hanging on the cross, was playing out on my television all week with Pope Francis's visit to the United States. I felt united with Jesus in suffering. As I watched the Roman Catholic masses and looked at the crucifix ever before me on television, Jesus' prayer from the cross once again became my mantra: *Into your hands, I commit my spirit.*

I read verse 3 from Psalm 27 that spoke to my heart: *Though an army besiege me, my heart will not fear; though war breaks out against me, even then will I be confident.*

As I read it, I thought of the national anthem: *...and the rockets' red glare, the bombs bursting in air...* and this nasty battle underway within my own body. I had been thinking of the sensations as fireworks, but maybe this really was a battle. Maybe rockets and bombs were a metaphor for this chemotherapy that was destroying the enemy of cancer. Maybe I really was in combat.

I pulled out construction paper and began to tear it up. I felt determined and angry, as though I was preparing for battle. I chose red paper to illustrate the rockets bursting overhead, then black paper to represent the darkness of evil. I could feel the drumbeats of war going on within me. Quickly I fashioned a crudely fashioned heart out of pink paper to represent the love of God. It became the centerpiece, and within the heart, I placed a picture of a sleeping baby. I began to feel peaceful. Something tense relaxed within me. The infant slept, unaware and unmoved by all the turmoil and hoopla going on around her. I heard a voice within whisper to me, "The battle is mine."

This was not the first time I had known hardship. There had been other times —the death of my parents and sister and beloved friends, the time Forrest lost his job, the move from Houston to Ft. Worth, the fear I felt in seminary taking exams, the years of chaos when our home was under construction. I don't know if any of us is immune from suffering in this life. What I had learned was to find that place of peace that lives deeply within me. We all have it. My task and challenge were not to get caught up in all the anxiety and fear of this life-threatening disease but to capture the serenity of a sleeping baby.

The words of Jesus to his disciples at their last supper together ministered to my heart: *Peace I leave with you; my peace I give you...Do not let your hearts be troubled and do not be afraid.* Peace is a great gift of faith. When my anxiety level and frustration began to rise, and I knew it would happen again and again, when the bombs would hit close in my mind, I imagined this tranquil little baby completely at peace, and it helped. I felt a shift in my spirit from turmoil to peace.

BEAUTY

One thing I ask of the Lord, this is what I seek; that I may dwell in the house of the Lord all the days of my life, to gaze upon the beauty of the Lord and to seek him in his temple. (Psalm 27:4)

Psalm 27 became the perfect psalm for me as I worked through the cancer. I think it would work well for anyone who struggles with life at times—those times when it seems like everything becomes stacked against you and you're not sure which way to turn. You know, those periods in life when everything changes to bad in a matter of seconds. Your husband says, "I don't love you anymore. I want a divorce. There's someone else." The economy tanks in a day, and you lose most of your retirement plan. You find your spouse dead when you wake up in the morning. You discover your child is on drugs. Everything is normal—you're going about your life like you always do, and then BAM! Your life and everything in it change on the spot.

My life changed dramatically with one mammogram. I was searching for a new normal. This was the verse I was dealing with in October, after my second round of chemotherapy: *One thing I ask of the Lord, this is what I seek; that I may dwell in the house of the Lord all the days of my life, to gaze upon the beauty of the Lord and to seek him in his temple.* I read verse 4 several times, and the phrase that sparkled for me was "beauty of the Lord."

To connect God's beauty with a church, to do that very literally, is a stretch for me as a Presbyterian. Our sanctuaries are austere. We ripped all the pretty statues and decorations out centuries ago during the Reformation. People went through with clubs and started swinging, destroying every trace of Roman Catholicism in their wild-eyed fury.

Down came the painted statues, the flickering candles, the ornate altarpiece, and the stained-glass windows that told the stories of the Bible. Out with the holy water basins and the little wooden booths where people confessed their sins to the priest. No more tabernacles where the host is kept.

In John Calvin's world, the sanctuaries were austere—nothing on the walls, no statues, no kneeling or body movement. Everything became focused on the pulpit, the centerpiece of nearly every Protestant church where the word of God is heard and proclaimed.

When I thought of "the beauty of the Lord," the first thing in my mind was not a sanctuary where Protestants like myself worship. If there is any beauty at all in a Presbyterian sanctuary, it is in its simplicity. There is very little to distract anyone from the sermon, other than zoning out and engaging in one's thoughts. Oh, there is beauty in the people who gather there, but that does not always bring with it a sense of transcendence, not for me anyway. A worship service can be beautiful, but that's not what surfaces when I think about the beauty of the Lord.

When I think of God's beauty, I think of being out of doors in nature—experiencing things like a tranquil lake framed with dark, Christmas-like trees or the snow-capped mountains of the Rockies. Or maybe a rainforest in Costa Rica with howler monkeys jumping around in the tops of the tall trees. I remember going to Maine once and sitting outside on a wooden picnic bench at dusk. The darkening sky blended with the murky-looking sea in a way that seemed seamless. It surrounded us, and we became one with it.

As I sat with this passage of Scripture, what came to me was the image of a glorious, multi-colored sunset streaking across the early evening sky, especially those sunsets as I have known them at our little farm in Shiner, Texas. They sometimes take my breath away by their dazzling, show-stopping glory. They lift me into the presence of God. The cows grazing in the grass, the vibrant flower vines growing on the fences, and the trees standing tall and stately bearing witness to the majesty of God. They become for me a sacred, holy temple for the divine.

I turned to my art. I glued a glittery gold piece of paper to my journal, then tore red, orange and pink construction paper. I layered them on top of the gold, and voila! My own personal, living sunset recorded for all time! What can be more beautiful than a sunset flung across a golden sky?

With my dominant hand, I asked the sunset, "What is your message to me?" The nondominant hand scrawled out these words: *You are beautiful too, Pat, and I love you. I am healing you through your art and your blog, and you will have a new ministry with lots of energy.* I asked my sunset, *"What do you need from me?"* Its answer? *Pay attention, little one. Keep your heart open to wonder. It will never fail you.* So there.

Yes, the world is on fire! A steady appetite of news makes us crazy with all the turmoil and dissension. Every day brings a new tragedy somewhere, and there is great angst and anxiety from every quarter. I heard the call to get out there and make a difference, even though I was secluded at home. The Christian faith means more than just "Jesus and me." I get that. But starting my devotional life with a loving process, art and journaling, and focusing on beauty that day enabled me to be present to the world in a way that I could not be without it. After all, I was battling a dreaded disease that was trying to kill me. Cancer stalked me and trumpeted its cry at every turn. Without the constant encouragement of my quiet time with God, I would have gone under.

If the inner voice leads one to the love of God, oneself, and others, that is a good thing. After all, Jesus said those were the great commandments. If listening to that voice and receiving it into one's spirit brings with it the gift of inner peace or joy or any of those things associated with the Holy Spirit, then it is a good thing.

Maybe it's God. Maybe not. But spiritual practices ground me and help me, and I am going to pay attention to that. For me, it became the essence of my transformation.

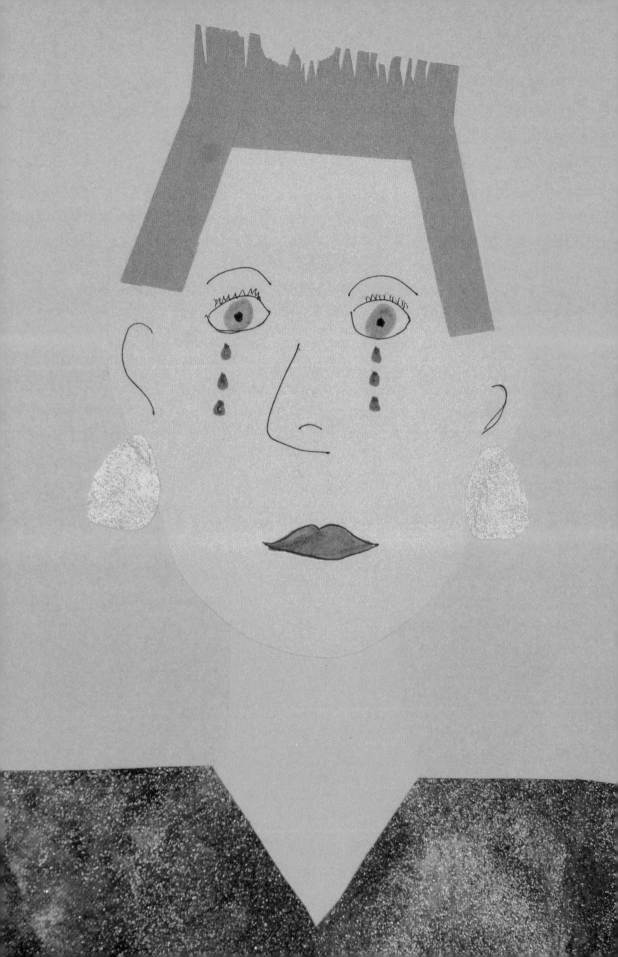

THE BLAHS

He will hide me in his shelter in the day of trouble;
he will conceal me under the cover of his tent. (Psalm 27:5)

*T*hree weeks into my first chemotherapy, I lay folded on the couch as tears streamed down my face. I wanted my mother, who had been dead for more than 50 years. Sadness overwhelmed me. In my mind's eye, I kept seeing a picture in my mind of a little girl crying.

I had planned to go on a trip to New Orleans that day, get on a bus with good friends, and have myself a grand old time. They would still have a grand time. Maybe I would hear about it when they got back. Maybe not. Meanwhile, I would lie there curled on the end of my brown couch in the living room like I did every day.

I had also canceled that wonderful cruise to Puerto Rico and the Virgin Islands. Dr. Turturro said, "You cannot travel until you finish this course of chemotherapy. You have no immune system. You must take your temperature every day because a fever of more than 100.5 degrees requires a trip to the emergency room. A simple infection can kill you. Cruise ships are notorious breeders of infections. To go on that trip is to risk death." They didn't mince words over at MD Anderson.

I had grown numb on the inside. There was no rah-rah that day. No big cheerleading and victory talks. No warrior imagery. I did not feel like a warrior. I had a case of the blahs, flat and lifeless.

Late Sunday evening a great pain attacked my back where there was still a wound from the bone marrow biopsy on my hip. It almost crippled me with pain. That's why nurses tell patients to take Claritin® before the Neulasta® injection, the shot that raises our white blood count. For some reason that allergy medicine stops the pain. I forgot. It was hard to remember everything. I made a vow not to forget the next time. The pain took me down a notch.

I remembered the word of the ancient Psalm: *Hear, Oh Lord, when I cry aloud!* (Psalm 27:7). It became my mantra for the day. When I looked further at Psalm 27, I was taken with verse 5: *He will hide me in his shelter in the day of trouble; he will conceal me under the cover of his tent.* Right then the phrase "cover of his tent" jumped at me. I imagined what that would be like to be hidden under the cover of God's tent. First, I thought of all the sparkly things I associate with heaven—streets of gold and jewels and everything fresh and shiny. I imagined a glittery, golden tent set up amid all that glory. I cut and pasted a representation of a tent from gold paper and glued it in my journal.

Then I thought about it. Where might God pitch a tent on Earth? Would it be a full church on a Sunday morning with a grand organ? Would it be someplace beautiful like the Canadian Rockies or the Austrian Alps? Those are the most beautiful places I had ever seen. God is beauty after all. Wouldn't God go somewhere beautiful?

The more I wondered, the more I began to think that God's place on Earth would be with all those who suffer and who are oppressed. Goodness, there were a lot of choices there—war-ravaged countries, victims of all manner of oppression, those suffering from mental illness. Finally, I thought that if God had a tent on Earth, it would be among refugees. I was still haunted by the picture of a little child whose dead body lay on the shore after a boatload of refugees tried to escape Syria. The condition of the refugee camps was horrible. It would be hard to top them when it came to human misery.

I thought of my time as pastor of St. Stephen Presbyterian Church in Houston. A friend from Rwanda was working with African refugees from Burundi and the Congo. She asked if she could bring them to church for International Women's Day and have me speak to them. We invited them for worship, church school, and lunch. "Don't give them much meat," she counseled. "They are not used to it. It will make them sick. Just put a little in the rice, more like a flavoring."

The refugee women arrived, dressed colorfully in reds, oranges, purples, and other colors fashioned into long dresses made of African fabrics. During the Sunday school hour, they spoke of their lives in refugee camps. Some had lost their children and other family members with no idea where any of them were. They spoke of long, hot days with nothing to do, cramped living conditions, brawls and fights, and little food or medical care. They were all eager to leave the camps, but now they were having trouble adjusting to life in America —the traffic, the food, electrical devices, transportation. They were plagued by illiteracy, language barriers, and no marketable skills. The stories broke our hearts.

We fed them lunch, then gave them poster board, stacks of magazines, scissors, and glue sticks. "Think of your new life," I told them. "What are your hopes and dreams now that you have left the refugee camps and come to America? What is your heart's desire?" The Rwandan interpreter translated the instructions into their native language. We all began clipping images as we sat together at long white tables—the African refugees and the American women from my Texas church.

Soon they were finished, and everyone wanted to share their work. They took turns talking about their posters. What all our African sisters wanted was a life free from war. They pasted beautiful pictures of nature onto those boards to illustrate peace. Others left blank space to describe their longing for a life without danger. Only a few pictures dotted their boards, and these illustrated a home, a car, and a happy family. Nearly all of them had a picture of Oprah, yet no one knew who she was. One woman had only one picture, and it was one of Oprah. Through the translator, she explained, "This woman is happy, and if I am happy, then none of the other things matter."

From that day forward, I thought of those refugee women whenever I thought about tents—the African women and the people who were then streaming out of Syria. I had begun this day with such incredible sadness and half folded up on my couch, but then I remembered those African women and their

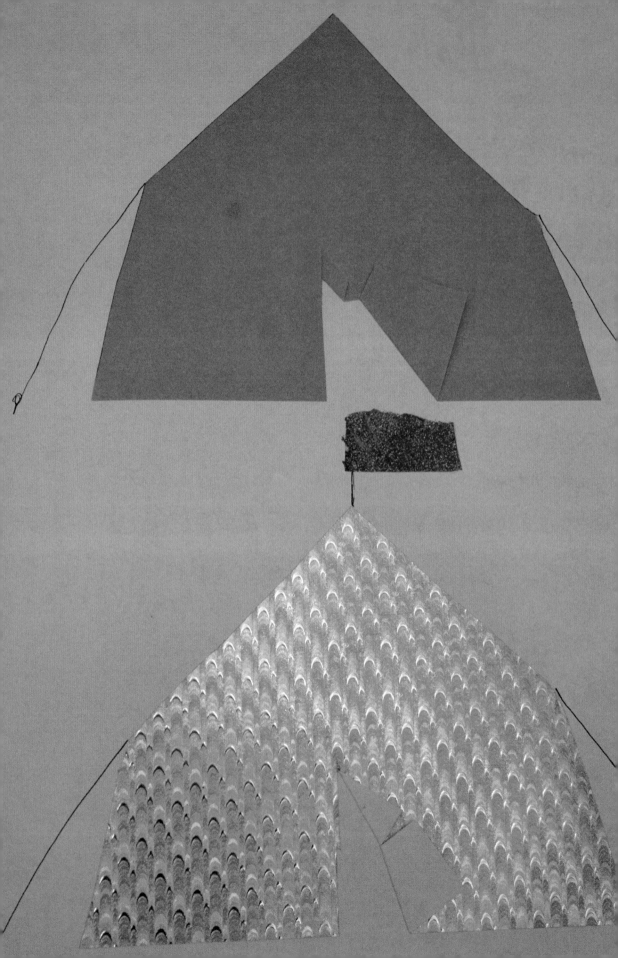

experiences in the refugee tents. Recalling their stories brought me to a higher place. God is with all those who suffer, and God was with me in mine. I felt a solidarity with people all over the world who are dealing with terrible things, things much worse than stage 4 cancer. Remembering them took the focus off me and connected me to others. I was grateful that I was not alone in the trials of life, even though my hardship paled in comparison to theirs. It is a strange and unusual fellowship among those who suffer, a fellowship no one wants. A kinship develops. It felt good to think of others besides myself.

HAIR

I knew my hair would fall out. Everyone knows that. It's a given. We've all seen the bald, pasty white heads. I never really liked my hair anyway. It had a mind of its own. Elegant women have sleek, straight, shiny hair. Think of Princess Diana or Kate Middleton. My hair had never looked like that except for the first hour or two after I had been to the beauty salon. Most often my hair was curly and unmanageable and frizzed in the Houston humidity. It frequently looked like straw until I cut it, but then there were these cowlicks sticking straight up, and no amount of coaxing would bring them down.

Still, the idea of awakening with clumps all over my pillow or seeing batches of hair in the shower drain freaked me out. I mean, I cannot even think about that without feeling disgusted! Some people get anxious about spiders. I cannot abide stray hairs on countertops or anywhere in the bathroom. Ugh! I decided to be proactive. Summoning all the courage I could muster, I texted my favorite hairdresser, Lindy, and asked if she could come cut my hair. We agreed on a time, 7:30 the next Friday evening.

Here's how I see the hand of God in all of this and where I see all the prayers and kind thoughts working. Shortly after texting her, I received some lovely blonde wigs in the mail, the gift of Forrest's cousin who had finished her cancer treatment. On Friday our son Trevor texted that our granddaughter and her boyfriend were in town for the weekend, and they were on the way, with dinner. On a lark, I texted my daughter and asked if she would like to participate via FaceTime. She and her beau were having dinner at a restaurant in Illinois but enthusiastically responded. My granddaughter held the cell phone while Lindy chopped away. Sipping their drinks and eating dinner, my daughter and her partner were an important part of everything. So was Lindy's husband who had come along with her.

What could have been a dreadful, tearful experience was transformed into a fun beauty salon party in my family room. I was surrounded by the people who love me the most. We told raunchy jokes, laughed a lot, and had a wonderful time. Best of all, I LOVED my new hairdo that was short and perky.

One morning not long after that, I awakened with pain in my scalp—different splashes of pain all over my head. It hurt! This was a new pain, a little like the exploding rockets, but only underneath my scalp. It lasted about 30 minutes or so, then went away. I got out of bed and took a shower. Then I noticed that my hair was falling in the drain. This was it—the sight of hair all over the place where it did not belong, the thing I did not want to see. It made me feel nauseous. This was the week before the second chemotherapy treatment. I knew I was losing my new, short hairdo, right on schedule.

I called Lindy again. She came right over. When she arrived, I placed a dining room chair in the middle of the floor in my family room, then sat on it. Lindy covered me with the black silken cape, then stood behind me. She put a comb through my hair and watched it fill up with my falling hair. She paused slightly and looked at my daughter Emi who was in town. I said, "Don't shave it completely. Leave about one-fourth of an inch." For some reason, the idea of shaving my head bald was too uncomfortable. Right after that, I heard the electric shaver. I sat very still, stoic as usual, unfeeling, numb. Lindy worked while Emi watched.

Emi would later say that she will never forget the look of love in Lindy's eyes as she worked and offered me words of encouragement. "Oh, you have such a nice shape to your head! So many people don't. You don't have dents or bumps or anything. It's really nice!" Emi said, "You look great bald!" Lindy told me later she cried all the way home.

I never felt sad about losing my hair. Quite frankly, I was glad not to have to mess with it. As far as I was concerned, a big problem had been eliminated, and I looked forward to what the new crop of hair might be after chemotherapy. It would be good to start over.

I put on one of the pretty caps I had bought to cover my bald head. Throughout the day, the one-fourth inch of hair all over my head continued to fall out, but in the cap. It started to itch after a while, and I shook it out over the trash can. I had to repeat that process all during the day. I had more hair than I realized! By the next day, I was completely bald.

I surveyed myself in the mirror, turning to the right and to the left with a hand-held mirror so I could see the sides and the back. "Hmmm," I thought. "That's not so bad. I can live with this!" I did not mind having a bald head or being seen in public with it, but it was cold. There is a purpose to having hair on one's head.

The thing I had dreaded in the beginning, the gross part of losing all my hair and seeing it everywhere, became a piece of cake. It was no biggie. It was just another step in the adventure. I didn't have to worry anymore about what it would be like. Now I knew. I had endured what many consider to be the toughest part of cancer and came through it just fine. "If I can survive this hard thing," I thought, "then I can survive other hard things... Baby steps," I told myself, "One day at a time." That's how I would get through this whole cancer thing, whatever the outcome. I knew I was loved. I knew I was not alone, and knowing that gave me confidence that some kind soul would be there to help at every turn.

FLOATING

Hide me in the shadow of your wings. (Psalm 17:8)

O n the last day of her pregnancy, my friend Rachel came to see me and gave me a gift. It was a book of poems that had ministered to her during a health crisis. One of the poems in the lovely book, authored by Denise Levertov, spoke to me and triggered a beautiful memory of a time in Galveston. Several of my girlfriends and I rented a beach house for the weekend and took some needed time off. One afternoon, I floated in the water for hours and allowed the waves to carry me further and further from our house. I felt safe and buoyed, upheld by a large and gentle force. I sensed a oneness with the water, the sky, the birds in the air and with all of creation. It was a magical and mystical space. That image came to me as I read this poem by Denise Levertov in the early morning hours before the sun rose. Here it is:

> *As swimmers dare to lie face in the sky and water bears them,*
>
> *As hawks rest upon air and air sustains them,*
>
> *So would I learn to attain freefall and float into Creator Spirit's deep embrace,*
>
> *Knowing no effort earns that all surrounding grace.*

Most often, I have used the method of *lectio divina* or divine reading, with Scripture, but on this day, I decided to use that process with this poem. As I read it through, the word that spoke to me was the word "float." I remember that day of floating in the Galveston sea. Were there other meanings that I could ponder?

I thought of birds as they soar through the air, of clouds in a pretty turquoise sky, of colored leaves falling to the ground in the fall. I didn't think long about airplanes. They are too noisy! I thought of God's natural world.

Then I asked myself the question: *What would it mean for me to float in the embrace of God?* I thought it would be a place of absolute safety and trust. There would be neither fear nor anxiety. There would be perfect peace. I would feel light in my spirit, not burdened by anything, nor worried about my life or my children, or the world, or anything else.

The third movement of the *lectio divina* process asks you to make the chosen word or phrase one's prayer. I visualized myself floating in the warm water of Galveston, and I asked God to bring me to that place of perfect peace within myself. I wanted to feel lighthearted, not burdened by the world's problems or my own. I lifted people and situations in prayer, and as I did, I saw each one of them floating into God's embrace. Most of all, I wanted to be able to trust like I did in that day in Galveston, trust God to keep me afloat in this world.

The fourth movement is to listen, to rest gently in the presence of God. The only thing that came to my consciousness was the phrase, "Be still." This is a phrase from Psalm 46 that carries the meaning of "Relax!" or "Turn loose! Let go!" The words were right on target. I held too many things too tightly. Now I let them go. The cancer, the treatment, everything floated away. I felt lighter.

If there is time, like when I had active cancer and did nothing but stay at home all day, I could take the process of *lectio divina* a step further and illustrate it. This connects the verbal with the visual, joining both the right and left brains. It helps me remember it better.

I pasted a blue piece of paper in my journal that I purchased for artwork to remind me of the bright blue sky in Galveston that day long ago. I felt seamless with the water. I covered half of the page with some glitter paint to resemble the sun that shone on the water and seemed to make it sparkle. I cut out a figure to represent my lily-white body and placed it in the water as I imagined it from that time long ago, floating and filling with perfect peace and love. Just looking at the picture and remembering that day filled me all over again with wonder and love.

To go even further into the work, I decided to journal with my Galveston image by using Lucia's four questions:

Who are you? *I am your peaceful self, enjoying God's world.*

How are you feeling? *Perfect! I do not have a care in the world! Can't you see I am floating and happy?*

What is your message to me? *You need to turn loose more often. Take better care of yourself. I have called you by name. You are mine.*

What do you need from me? *I need you to remember that I am leading and guiding you. I know what is best for you. When you come to peace in my love, you hear my voice. I have a beautiful future for you. Learn to float more often.*

When I had finished this, I was filled with great peace. I felt loved.

Now, whenever I look at this picture, I remember those three experiences—the day when I literally floated in the Gulf of Mexico, the day Rachel brought me the book of poetry, and the day God spoke to me through this simple kindergarten art.

The work of prayer, memory, cutting and pasting, and then dialoguing with my image kept me grounded, maintained my serenity, and enabled me to go through the next hard thing. I was grateful.

FEAR

When I was first diagnosed with cancer, I cried a little every day because I wanted my mother. Cancer has a way of taking you to what is most primitive and basic in your life. With laser-like focus, it strips the wheat from the chaff —teaching what is primal and what is true. It stripped me to my foundations. Lately, I had been sitting around looking normal, but inside I was 4 years old, the age I was when my father died.

I was afraid. Since the first chemotherapy, I was still living with what seemed like the Fourth of July in my body. Bottle rockets were shooting through my veins. Then came the Roman candle blasts, one after another in quick succession. I had been thinking this was the reaction to Prednisone®. Wrong. This was chemotherapy. Ugh! My new normal–maybe forever. Ever so gently, fear began to stalk me.

What if this gets worse?

What if the bad builds on the bad every time?

What if I really do lose all feeling in my extremities?

What if this never gets any better?

And finally, I don't think I can do this.

I picked up my prayer shawl and headed to the couch to assume a fetal position. This was a frequent body position those days—curled on a pillow on the end of my favorite couch wrapped in a shawl or a throw blanket. In that posture I felt held in the womb of God, like an infant in the uterus, surrounded.

Yes, I knew that God is love and that love is the only antidote for all those hidden feelings I don't like to show to the world—fear, self-loathing, shame, vulnerability, depression, you name it. Reclining on the couch and feeling alone and vulnerable, a quiet terror rose within me. I tried to imagine myself being held in the love of God and pulled the turquoise shawl up over my ears. I used to banish those hard feelings. I used to speak to myself in militaristic terms: *Soldier up! Stuff those troubling feelings down and get on with life! There is work to be done! Come on now, get over yourself! You can do this hard thing!* I never, ever had any mercy for myself. I have been a cruel taskmaster.

Lucia taught me to journal with those feelings, to draw them all out and to dialogue with them. But this day I was tired, exhausted, and weak. I could not muster the energy to do anything. I lay there on the brown leather-like couch, the sun streaming in through the windows and me swaddled in my turquoise throw. I could not think. My body trembled. I could only whisper a shallow prayer: *Help me.*

Not long after, maybe a few minutes, maybe even a few hours, I got a text from Susie, the friend who is a cancer nurse, the one who showed up the night

I had that horrific reaction to the chemotherapy surging through my veins in the hospital. "Can I come over?" she said. "Yes!" I texted in return.

When she arrived at my house in the afternoon, I was still in pajamas. I asked all my questions. She answered them all. "Yes, the bottle rockets are normal. Yes, it is the Fourth of July in your body. Yes, you are supposed to be tired, even this tired. Yes, you will burn up one minute, and then have chills and be freezing cold the next. Yes, yes, yes—all of this is normal." She is a powerful presence. When she speaks, no one disagrees with her. Finally, she told me, "You can do this." I believed her. When she walked in the door, she always brought hope.

After Susie left, I looked in my kindergarten art book where I had fashioned the sleeping child safe in the womb of God, even though she was surrounded by bursting rockets. I stared at her and felt the familiar shift within me—lighter, not anxious anymore. The words for prayer did not form in my heart—I was becoming less and less wordy now. I could gaze upon the infant's picture, though, and understand that God was holding me. I silently held the image in my lap and knew within that God heard and understood. I felt a powerful, divine connection between God and me that morning. Later, if history is any indication, I would become distracted and forget, but in that moment the primitive image gave me great peace.

The responses that came later on my Caring Bridge site upheld me and carried me through the rest of my day. Claire wrote, "Oh, say can you see by the dawn's early light...You carry the Fourth of July in your body—an embodiment of your independence from this tyrant called cancer. May those bottle rockets and Roman candles do their job well and free you completely from its attack." She gave me a way to re-frame the experience, and I was grateful.

Instead of the Fourth of July representing war, it became a symbol of victory in the end. So yeah, I was in a permanent state of celebrating our nation's independence in my body. Summer had faded, but in my spirit, I began to hear Sousa tunes. I saw in my mind the big Fourth of July parade in Shiner, Texas, where our farm is located and heard the music as the high school band marched down the street playing those big brass instruments. I saw the Veterans of

Foreign Wars carrying flags and riding in convertibles. "Perhaps," I thought, "I should download some Sousa tunes for those times I need to remember that victory over this disease is my goal."

UNFORGETTABLE PEOPLE

We came with our hair chopped off, bald heads, and bad wigs. Some like me rode in wheelchairs. Others walked in on their own steam. Some others trailed IV poles beside them as they walked. We were all in various stages of disease and treatment. You could tell the patients, if not by our physical appearance, by the white armbands we wore. Most of us came in twos, accompanied by our caregivers. Each of us battled the same disease and its consequences. We were all on a joint pilgrimage heading into the great unknown. Statistics say two out of three people with lymphoma will live another five years. My odds are more like 50-50 because the disease was so advanced and because of my age. The lymphoma lobby was always filled with people. Camaraderie developed as we waited, sometimes for hours at a time. The most frequent question I got was this: "Where are you from?" People come from all over the world to MD Anderson. I was blessed that MD Anderson was only a 5-minute drive from our home.

We waited, and then we waited some more. Our common joke was that the MD in MD Anderson stands for "most of the day." While we were sitting around, we gave each other tips, "You can park at the proton center for free, then take the shuttle over here. Saves you a lot on parking! $10 a day adds up!" As we talked, nurses barked out our names and alerted us when it was time to have blood drawn, then vital signs taken, and then finally the visit with the doctor. Noise filled the crowded reception area. Sometimes volunteers came by with a cart serving coffee and tea. Strategically placed aquariums, jigsaw puzzles, and televisions tried to keep us calm.

Since I had started chemotherapy, I had gone to MD Anderson every week. The first week was chemo, but the next two involved blood work and talking to the physician's assistant about side effects. Then I repeated the cycle until the month after I had completed six chemotherapy treatments. We were all in this together. Cancer is the great equalizer.

One morning after my routine appointment, I waited outside next to a big, burly soybean farmer from Kansas while Forrest went to get the car. The farmer had a multi-colored beard down to his belly and wore sunglasses with yellow lenses. My new friend had parked at the proton center and was awaiting the shuttle. "I know where the proton center is," I told him. "My husband went there for prostate cancer."

"I bet he don't leak, do he?"

"No," I said, "he doesn't leak."

"I shoudda come here for that when I had it. Now I got this esophageal stuff, and it's all out of whack!" The shuttle pulled up, he said goodbye, and he and his wife boarded.

I met dozens of people, and some of them I will not soon forget. Another who lives in my memory is a young man I think of as "that guy." I never knew his name. I have never seen him again. We were having blood drawn at the same time one Monday morning. I could barely sit up in my wheelchair. This was the week following my first chemotherapy treatment, and I was tired. I know tired. I have been tired most of my life, but this kind of fatigue was beyond anything I had ever experienced. "That guy" was a spunky guy, maybe about 35 years old. He stood about five feet, eight, and was muscular and blond. He wore a big smile on his face. He was wearing blue jeans, like a lot of people do at MD Anderson.

He told me to take Claritin® before the Neulasta® injection, which is given to boost one's white cell count. It helps to prevent infections later on. "Man, oh man, that is the worst backache you will ever have if you don't!" he said. He was in his fifth treatment cycle and radiated positive energy. My, he lit up that little room by his very presence. I would not have been surprised if he had taken off in a jog down the hallway.

He told the phlebotomists (we called them vampires) that he needed to finish at MD Anderson as quickly as he could because he had to go to work. "You just had chemotherapy and you're going to work?" I asked incredulously. "Yeah," he said, "it gets to me if I'm around the house too long." He took off, and I saw him later near the infusion center—strong gait, practically jogging and with the same big smile still on his face and full of energy and optimism.

That guy blew me away when it came to how a person can feel when undergoing treatment for cancer. Before him, I figured I would feel awful, nauseous and full of neuropathy (loss of feeling in the extremities) for my entire cycle of chemo. I felt like a perfect victim. This terrible disease had crippled me physically and emotionally. But "that guy" radiated good health, as though nothing was wrong in his body. In that brief encounter, without ever really speaking of it, his actions showed me a better way to do chemo. I was focusing on all the negatives of treatment, and they were legion, but he was focused on his job and his family and on a way to live a productive life during it. He was not sitting around quietly feeling like a martyr and feeling sorry for himself. He was being proactive, staying fit and positive.

Cancer did not define him. Other things like his job and family did. I wanted to be like him. I did not want to be a victim anymore. Yeah, I had cancer, but I was more than the cancer. I made a vow to live with hope.

Later that same morning, I had an oncology massage. When I checked in to the integrative medicine center, there was a little sign on the check-in pad. It said simply, "Be strong. You never know who you're inspiring!!" I thought of that guy and smiled to myself. A chance encounter had made all the difference.

THE PRAYERS OF THE PEOPLE

Week Two of chemotherapy brought a new level of fatigue. I had been warned about it on the day I began treatment. Ly, the physician's assistant to Dr. Turturro, had been very matter-of-fact. "Your blood counts will go down," she explained. "When that happens, you will feel tired, more tired than you have ever been, but it's not permanent. You will feel much better the third week as your blood counts begin to rise. Then we will take you down again."

Boy, was she right! I had never known this kind of tired. It felt as though someone had poured concrete through my veins. Every movement required effort. Resistance preceded even the simplest of tasks, like walking across the floor or bending over to pick up something. I was the tin man without any oil. I was a monument in the park. This was my new norm. Inside, my spirit longed to be free, but I was paralyzed from soaring. The struggle to move became too great. I spent most of my time on the couch. I was hoping to take a shower that day in October but could not do it. I would have to use more perfume.

I remembered a story from the gospel of Mark where Jesus was off somewhere teaching, surrounded by a big crowd. Some people brought a paralyzed friend to him, and they could not make it through the crowds. Instead, they cut a hole through the roof and lowered the guy down on a mat right in front of Jesus. Jesus forgave his sins and healed him, and the guy stood up and walked out. Of course, that freaked everybody out. Jesus is the all-time master of freaking everybody out.

I liked that image, though, because I was as debilitated, almost, as the guy on the mat. I was helpless and vulnerable that week, unable to do even a simple thing like get into a shower. In this rather weird condition, so foreign from my normal way of being, I could only lie there and allow my friends to hold me before the presence of God. The prayers meant everything to me.

The evening before I began the first round of chemotherapy, my colleague group gathered in my living room with communion. Noelie had designed a little prayer service and printed it on a bulletin. She said she didn't want anything slipshod; she wanted it to be reverent and nice. My Presbyterian clergy friends surrounded me; they read Scripture and repeated the ancient words preceding the sacrament. We all shared a piece of bread, leftover from worship at one of their churches that morning. We drank grape juice, or wine, I cannot remember, and they prayed for me. For the life of me, I do not remember what they prayed. I remember only that I was surrounded by their love, and their gentle prayers blessed me. The cancer was spreading throughout my body. My blood marrow was full of it. I was at stage 4. Stage 4 usually means that death is imminent. I thought a lot of my friends were thinking that, even though they were not saying it.

I did not think I was about to die, however, although I did anticipate some pretty good suffering. I wondered what would happen to my fingernails. One friend told me to keep them in ice water during every chemotherapy treatment to prevent weird things from happening to them—discoloration, ridges, and I don't remember everything else. Some people had neuropathy in their hands and feet. I knew one person who was still unable to button or unbutton a blouse because of the numbness in her fingers caused by chemotherapy.

The evening prayer with my friends felt good to my spirit though, and I began to ask other people who visited me to pray for me. Most people would say, "I am praying for you." To get them to pray out loud in my presence could be intimidating though. It's hard and embarrassing for someone to do that if one is not accustomed to public prayer.

An unforeseen event boosted my morale. Forrest and I owned a little rent house in Rosenberg, Texas, in a low-income part of town. The air conditioning went out in that house. The woman who had lived there for years found an air conditioning repairman who would replace the system for a fraction of the cost most people were asking. To begin working, he had to get a check from me for half the costs of replacement. The two guys who came to my house for the check were African-American Christians from an evangelical tradition.

I asked them to pray for me and pray they did. They prayed loud! They commanded Satan to "leave this woman alone" in no uncertain terms. They screamed at the devil. They pleaded for the blood of Jesus to cover me and asked in no uncertain terms that "no weapon formed against me would prosper."

Most of the Christians I hang out with don't pray that way. We are soft. We are sweet. We ask nicely, respectfully, for God to intervene and to help. We speak in traditional, gentle ways as we ask for the angels to surround the person, to protect him or her. We pray for love to prevail. It's like we are always hedging our bets in case the prayer isn't answered.

These black men were not that way. They prayed with AUTHORITY, as though they were Jesus himself. My goodness, how I loved it! My spirit soared right up there and wordlessly joined in. We made quite a scene in my living room— me sitting on the couch and them sitting in the red fabric recliner chairs and hollering at God and the devil alternatively. They were loud! It was great fun, moving even. I hated for it to end.

I have always thought that many African-Americans and Hispanics have the greatest faith among Christians. I think it is because so many of them have never had the resources that many privileged Anglos do. Anglos in my crowd have many ways to get their needs met. We often have more money. We are connected to channels of power. Often, we have health insurance and can go to the best doctors. We are privileged as we navigate this life. Some minorities often have only the resources of their faith, and that faith is large because of it. My own faith seems puny in comparison, even though I have advanced degrees. Sometimes it seems like the more educated we are, the further away we move from genuine faith. We get stuck in our heads.

Now I found myself in a place where a head-centered faith wasn't enough. I had stage 4 cancer, for God's sake! Philosophizing seemed worthless in this condition. I needed more than I could muster. The day the African Americans showed up in my red, sun-drenched living room and prayed for me, I indeed felt like the guy on the mat being lifted before Jesus. My spirit climbed right up to heaven with them. A surge moved through my body. I knew God was present, and I sensed an opening through which my spirit could rise, despite my wooden legs and body.

Prayer comforted me the most in going through the cancer experience. A group of young clergy journeying through European spiritual sites sent word to me that they had prayed for me the evening before. They had presented my name at a healing service at the Abbey in Iona, Scotland. A Muslim friend, whose nephew was making his pilgrimage to Mecca, e-mailed that his nephew was praying for my healing as he walked the sacred ground. Several Jewish friends lifted my name in their synagogues during Yom Kippur, the high holy day of Judaism. A Buddhist actor friend in Los Angeles prayed for my healing during a 3-hour, non-stop chant. And a friend's mother, visiting Philadelphia, lifted me in prayer during Pope Francis' historic papal mass in that city. Several people told me their churches were praying for me. Facebook posts, comments on the Caring Bridge website, e-mails, and cards in the mail told me that I was being held before God. This all meant the world to me. Knowing all this kept my spirits up and kept me going. I was grateful.

One of the ministers in my church asked after the chemo experience ended, "I wonder which one of your friends has the gift of healing. Which one of them said the words that resulted in your being cancer free?" I don't know. I don't know if it was one person or a thousand all together. I don't know if it was the African American men or the chemotherapy. My best guess is that it was everything working together—God's will, prayers from all traditions, modern medicine, loving friends and family, creative journaling, and my fierce determination to live.

Why does prayer "work" for some and not others? There's no good answer. I think God is good and wills the best whether we live or die. Cancer doesn't come from God. Why some are healed and others are not I can never say. No one can. What I know for sure is there are powerful lessons that can only be learned through suffering, whether one lives or dies. In my case, the knowledge that so many people were praying on my behalf comforted me in a way nothing else did. I felt supported and loved. I remain grateful for the profound gift of those prayers.

FRIENDSHIP

My friend had tears in her eyes as she presented it to me—a multi-sided former hat box now painted a dusky shade of blue. "It's for your blue days," Ann told me, "and comes with love and so many prayers." Someone had given one to a mutual friend's daughter to help her through the blue days of cancer, and she wanted to do that for me. "Phil (her husband) helped me wrap them," she added. I looked inside. Some two dozen individually wrapped packages were stuffed inside. A silver colored angel rested on top. Her love and gratitude overwhelmed me. How special to have a 45-year friendship! How tender to know that she and her husband thought of me as they wrapped each package individually!

"Some of them come from our history together," she told me, her eyes tearing up again as we remembered a kind woman we both loved who had died. "Her memento is buried deep inside the box." What rich friendships we had shared! What lessons we had learned from our own personal heroes of faith! How much I was blessed by people in the communities of faith where I had served!

For a girl like me whose parents died so young (my father died when I was 4 and my mother, when I was 17) being part of a faith community has given me roots and a sense of belonging. It has held noble virtues before me, helped me to grow in faith, and given me deep and beautiful friendships for 45 years.

I know there is a dark side to organized religion. I have seen it. I have lived through it. I probably caused some of it for other people. I have experienced hard seasons of church life and seen people devastated by them. Sometimes forgiveness has been slow to come, and sometimes it doesn't come at all and forms scars on our hearts. We are, after all, broken people. If the church were perfect, there would be no room for anyone! For me, the benefits outweigh the negatives.

My friend, Marcia, also came to visit and brought the gift of a canvas bag she had painted. A button pinned to its side read, "Cancer Sucks." A 25-year survivor of cancer, Marcia was the first to talk to me one-on-one about her experience with this awful disease. The conversation was so very helpful.

"It's the loneliness that's hard," Marcia told me. "You're surrounded by people who love you and who want to help, but you're the only one with cancer. You're the only one going through treatment." She also told me, "Once you're diagnosed, cancer steps front and center to the forefront of your life. It dominates everything!"

Boy, was that ever true! Cancer now overshadowed everything in our lives from my daily routine to the storage of medical supplies and conversation. Life those days, its entire focus, became cancer. I never wanted to be like the old people I remembered from childhood whose only topic was their disease and treatment, and yet here I was! That's all I talked about. That's all I wrote about. Pat Clark was officially a diseased old fart.

Because I was homebound, I found myself hungering for news from the outside world—not the events on television, but the goings on in peoples' lives. My friend, Jan, came to see me on her lunch hour. She brought news from the Red Mass at the cathedral downtown. The annual event that kicks off the judicial year, it was packed with Roman Catholic attorneys. Her words were vivid, and I could see in my mind the procession with Cardinal De Niro, the acolytes and priests, and the sensors preceding down the aisle. I examined the program and was fascinated by the discussion. She also attended the annual Matthew Linn retreat at the Cenacle, an event we usually experienced together. Jan is the only person I know, like me, who likes to sit on the front row and take vociferous notes. She shared them with me, the "Cliff Notes" from the Beatitudes retreat. My heart was warmed.

After Jan left, my Jewish "mother" Geri came over. "I don't pray," she told me, "but I can do other things." Indeed. Geri brought us the best matzoh ball soup I have ever eaten. Geri is a holdover from my news career, and after 40 years of joy and sadness, she still makes me laugh.

The most fun gift came from joy bringers Linda and Zita—more than a hundred pumpkin things, including foods and gifts. I laughed hard retrieving those gifts from an enormous basket. Who knew they made pumpkin Twinkies? They delivered a care package every single month that I was in treatment.

Comments left on my CaringBridge site often ministered deeply to me. One night my friend John left a beautiful message that bears repeating. As he talked about his daughter who is guiding them through yoga exercises, he wrote that they always ended the experience with a lovely prayer, repeating it over and over. It was simply this: *May I be filled with loving kindness. May I be peaceful and at ease. May I be happy.*

People asked repeatedly what they could do to help. Asking anyone for anything was difficult for me. I was used to giving, not receiving! I'm a minister all. I had never been through cancer and did not always know what I needed. Here is what helped:

- Facebook likes and comments, jokes and funny stories or pictures and videos.

- Text messages of encouragement and support.

- Reading my CaringBridge site where people had left either a heart or a comment.

- Short visits that included personal news stories from peoples' lives.

- Cards and notes, both handwritten and on the computer.

- Flowers.

- Nutritious food that was not sugary or processed.

- Prayer. (This one should be at the top of my list.)

- Watching movies or listening to music with friends. Remember, I spent almost every day alone in my house, and I am an extrovert.

- Easy-to-read, trashy novels.

It's one thing to be loved when I am on the top of the world. I am remembering my ordination, installations and farewells, and our 50th anniversary party when a huge number of people ignored the rainy weather and came to surround us with love. My cup truly overflowed on those days. I always wondered though if the love was conditional. Would they still love me if I screwed up or fell from grace or could not respond? Would they abandon me when I was helpless and powerless to give back? I had never been truly vulnerable as an adult, but now I was. My energy was in the toilet. I could not do most of the things I was accustomed to doing. Truly my days consisted of lying on the couch.

All the attention from my family and friends, the cards, the visits, and the online comments were overwhelming. Overwhelming! I got it. I felt the love. It was so very precious. It might have been the very best gift of having cancer.

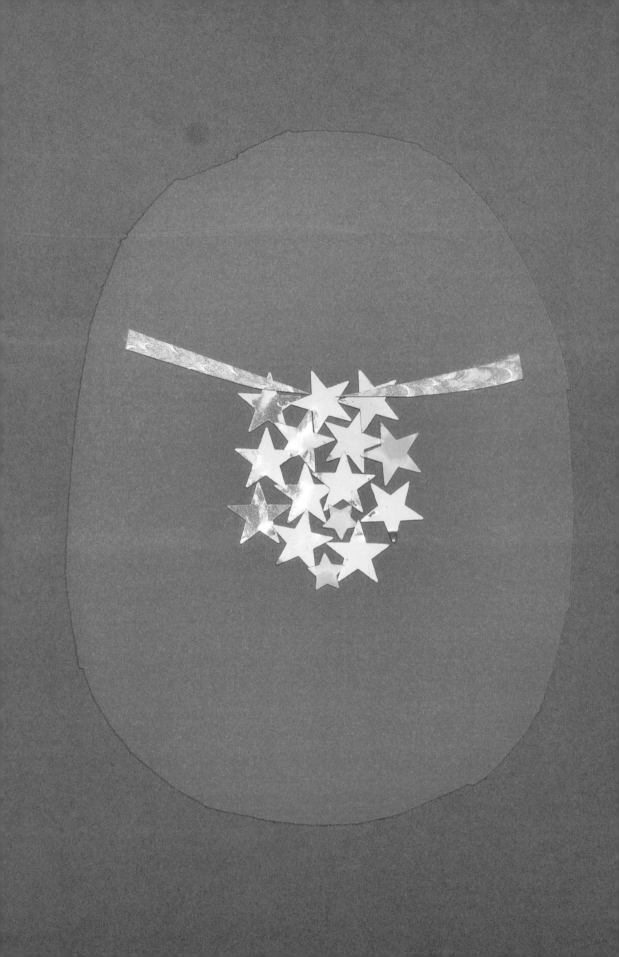

STARDUST

*For it was you who formed my inward parts, you knit me
together in my mother's womb.* (Psalm 139:13)

A striking image compelled me in the pre-dawn hours on November 8, 2015, while sitting on the couch with my art journal spread across my lap. It came from Psalm 139:13, and as I read it, the words drew me forward: *For it was you who formed my inward parts, you knit me together in my mother's womb.* Right away I imagined golden needles knitting stars. Isn't this something that scientists tell us—that we are all made of stardust? Such a striking visual image!

Imagine, the great knitter, working thoughtfully and lovingly, contemplating all the wonderful possibilities that can emerge from this glory as He/She works. Then we humans are born and grow up, and sometimes, maybe most of the time, we forget. I forget that I am created from stardust or maybe I fail to believe that. Some people never do learn that. And life becomes a storm that whirls and batters. Sometimes we never get off the ground because we don't acknowledge that we are, each one of us, created with divinity deep inside us. That's our core, our center.

During the time of rampant cancer trying to destroy me, God invited me to look deeply within to see the beauty, the hope, and the love with which I was fashioned. Despite all my efforts to cover it up, run away from it and hide, those stars still reside within me. My calling in that season became finding those divine sparks placed there before my birth, acknowledging them without giving into grandiosity, and allowing them to form my unfolding future.

The insights became a big deal for me that chilly November morning as I began my quiet time with God. The day before, I had received three separate prayer requests regarding three different young men. Each one of them found himself stuck in life, surrounded by barricades even though he was young. I had known all of them when I served as pastor of a church. I still prayed for the people in the churches where I served, and on this day those three guys were front and center.

One of them was a brilliant young man who suffered from radically low self-esteem. He came from a home where his father brutally abused him verbally nearly every day. He had turned to drugs to solve his problems, and although he was 25 or so, he could not hold down a job.

Another was an 18-year-old boy whose 16-year-old girlfriend turned up pregnant. Her parents forced marriage upon them. Here he was, young with no marketable skills, a family to support, and unable to get a job.

A third was a handsome young guy who loved music but had been diagnosed with paranoid schizophrenia. He was unable to hold a job for more than a few months at a time.

Doors did not open for any of these young men. They had lost vision. They could not see beyond the here and now, and the future loomed scary. They had no idea they were created from stardust. How could I help them from my place on the couch? I did not know, other than to pray for them. My situation seemed like theirs—trapped by life's obstacles.

Could their plight be like this cancer? None of us goes through life without great challenges. Mine was health. People could love me through it, but ultimately the journey was mine and mine alone. I could lecture those boys or listen to them for hours at a time, but ultimately, they would have to find their own strength.

I prayed for my young men that morning, and I prayed for myself:

For courage to stay on the right trail,

For hope to be born,

For wisdom along the way,

And for the grace to see the stars within and all around.

We can only see the stars in darkness. Like seeds planted in the ground, it takes darkness to germinate and to bring forth new life. Everyone must walk the road of trials at some point. We can resist them all we want, but if we will allow it, one day there will come a shift, a little ray of hope, a small green shoot. I believed it would come for these young men and also for me, and I prayed that it would come for all of those who are seeking.

THE HEM OF HIS GARMENT

You hem me in—behind and before;
you have laid your hand upon me. (Psalm 139:5)

*M*y grandmother Schuck lived with me my entire life until I left for college. We were roommates most of that time, sleeping on twin beds in the same bedroom. She was elegant and proper, I thought, because she wore high heeled shoes, stockings, makeup, and pearls every day of her life, even if she was scrubbing the floors. We took her to the beach once, and she waded out into the water in her stocking feet and her pearls.

The schools in Bisbee, North Dakota, only went to the third grade at the turn of the last century. Her father refused to let her go any further with her education because she was a girl and because there was too much women's work to be done on the farm. So Grandma Schuck became a seamstress even before she entered puberty and sewed garments for everyone in her family. She kept up that work well into her eighties and tried to disguise the shame of her lack of education.

Her Singer sewing machine sat in the corner of our bedroom—the one we shared. Every afternoon after all the chores were done, she would go into our bedroom and sew or do embroidery. I would lie on the chenille-covered bedspread and talk to her. "What was it like, Grandma, to live on a farm?"

She talked as she sewed. "It was hard," she would tell me. "We got up early because there was milking to be done. We had to have a big breakfast for the men when they came in. We cooked sausages we had made ourselves and fresh eggs that came from our chickens. We baked all our bread and served

69

jams and jellies we made from the fruit that grew in the summer. We canned everything. There was no store nearby."

She told me about the northern lights that would appear in the sky on those long, dark nights near the Canadian border. "We would see them late," she said, "and they would be all different colors, Patty. Sometimes they were green or red, or pink like, and sometimes they would be purple. They would dance across the sky all during the night. They were so beautiful."

Once she told me how they had crossed the plains in a covered wagon, fearful of encountering warring Indians. One night the Indians indeed camped with them. She added, "My mother did not sleep all night, not even a wink, because she was so afraid." The Indians were peaceful and left the next morning.

She sewed as she talked. I remember particularly how she would hem things by hand—dresses, skirts and blouses, curtains, everything! Whenever I think of a hem, I think of her and her sturdy, dedicated work that never unraveled. I don't know how to hem things. She never taught me. I have tried, but my hems never last. I don't have her skill.

The wind chill in North Dakota can be 40 degrees below zero in winter. No wonder she took to sewing! It seemed to me, listening to her stories, that they spent the entire summer getting ready for winter—planting gardens, harvesting them, and canning all the produce. Without having television or electronics of any kind and living in tiny houses, there was not much else for a woman to do besides sew in winter. And sew she did. She made all of my clothes for years, and all of her hems stayed in place.

The hem story that I came to love, however, I found in Psalm 139:5 where it is used as a verb. It reads, *You hem me in—behind and before; you have laid your hand upon me.* In Hebrew, the word "hem" is a word of great force. It means closed in, surrounded, confined, held close, hemmed in without being able to escape.

What we know from other places in Scripture is that God is love and light and healing and everything good. I began to imagine the healing that could happen inside God's hem, surrounded and held with love and light.

What a wonderful, wonderful place to be, held inside the hem of God, the place of radiance and healing.

On that morning, when I was in the midst of chemotherapy, and all my hair had fallen out, and I had hot flashes and then cold flashes, and muscle cramps and all the uncomfortable things that come from cancer treatment, this image of the hem came to me. I imagined Grandma sitting on her bench and hemming, and I thought, "Wow! I don't have to reach out for God in my exhausted state. I simply know that I am held and surrounded 24 hours a day, 7 days a week, in the healing hem of God's garment."

I remembered the rest of the good news: We all are. Whether we feel it or whether we don't, we are all held in the healing love of God. The promise of Scripture is this: God will never turn loose of us. The Apostle Paul wrote to the Romans centuries ago this truth that still stands: *For I am convinced that neither death nor life, neither angels nor demons, neither the present nor the future, nor any powers, neither height nor depth, nor anything else in all creation, will be able to separate us from the love of God that is Christ Jesus our Lord.* (Romans 8:38-39)

We are each held in the hem of divine love, and that marvelous love will never let us go.

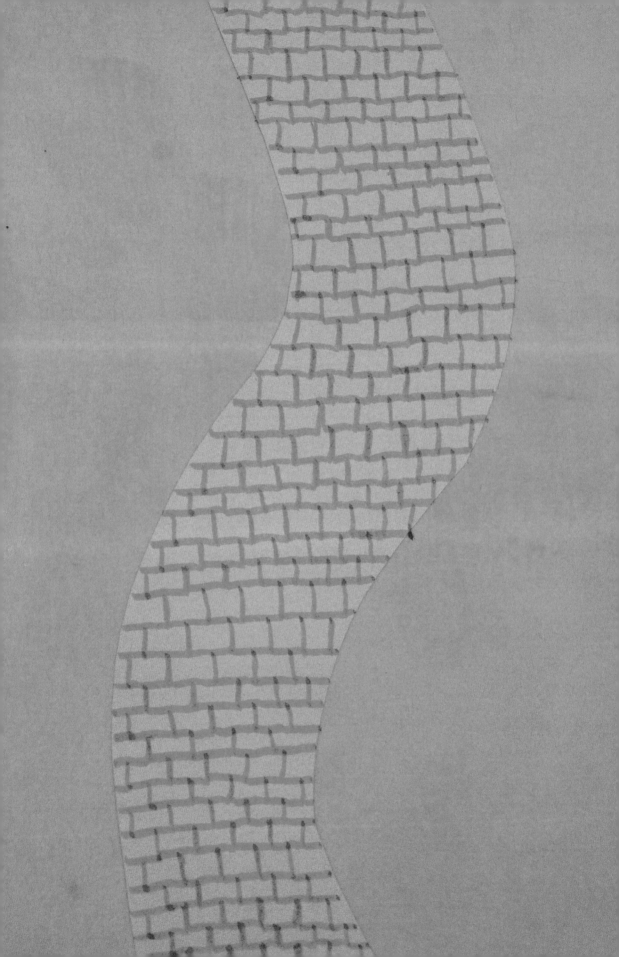

THE YELLOW BRICK ROAD

Teach me your way, O Lord, and lead me on a level path because of my enemies. (Psalm 27:11)

By mid-October 2015, I had been at this chemotherapy business about a month. I was weary of being a grownup. My concentration was shot. I could not read much or carry on intelligent conversations. People would talk about science or other heady topics, and I did not even try to listen. My mind zoned out. It was like I punched the delete button. I might have looked engaged. I might have seemed to follow along. But I was nowhere around in my head. I had gone to overwhelm and wiped my slate clean.

I reminded myself of people in my former churches who were in the beginning stages of dementia. Especially the Southern ladies. They would be oh so pleasant and make appropriate comments like, "Oh, I see!" or smile at the right times. In their minds, they were somewhere else, like I was in chemotherapy. It required too much effort to follow along.

People dropped off or sent me books. They looked interesting. In earlier times I could read a book a day. With chemo, I would read a paragraph or two and have no idea what I had just read. I quickly lost interest. I thanked people profusely. Stacks of books that were never opened piled up. It was no use trying to read. I knew what would happen. I quit trying. I reminded myself that one day the treatment would be over, and then I could read. I remembered the tests I took in school that said I was brilliant. Ha! They should have seen me in my cancer season. I felt I was borderline for any intelligence quotient at all!

If the television was on, I could not follow along. I never cared much for television anyway, so it was no big loss. It was simply too hard to focus on anything besides myself and my immediate needs, like being hot or cold. That happened all day long. Or being hungry or thirsty.

Even my prayer life suffered. The words didn't form in my head. Most days "Help!" was about all I could muster. Sometimes I called other people's names to mind, like my children and grandchildren, but mostly my prayer life was reduced to only a few words. I spent my days lying on the couch and looking out my living room windows. The French panes needed to be washed, but I didn't care. A lot of housekeeping chores needed to be done. I noticed them but did nothing. Most days it was too difficult even to sit up in a chair. I did enjoy company and could carry on conversations while lying on the couch.

In my dreams at night, I was still organizing the world. I did problem-solving, took care of people, and made decisions. I was active and dispensed information. I was busy, busy, busy and full of energy, a woman on the move. Then I awakened exhausted in the morning. It was difficult to organize the world every night! I would lie on the sofa in a fetal position–bald and weary from too little sleep. I pulled my turquoise throw up over my shoulder; my mind was blank. I had no focus. I could only lie there. A slug covered in turquoise chenille.

The sun rose, its pink and gold fingers streaming through the sky. *Will I rise like that?* I wondered as I moved to a recliner chair next to the couch and pulled out my journal. Nothing much came. I sat. I waited. *What would my life look like if I didn't just lie here?* Maybe I could have done a little more around the house. Dust shrouded every surface. Maybe I would have cooked something. Maybe I could have brought some order to the piles of books and articles on my table or done some rearranging. No, none of that was an option. Everything overwhelmed me.

I remembered the burden of the doctor's medical instructions. I could not go outside. Germs might cause an infection that could land me in the hospital because I had no immune system. No flossing, no pedicures, no being in public. Everyone who came into the house had to wash their hands, and nobody entered who had a cough or a runny nose. Even if I could have gone somewhere, I had no energy to do anything. Fatigue crippled me. If I was not careful, I beat myself up.

I found my Bible, the one held together with duct tape, and begin to search for Psalm 27. My eyes landed on verse 11: *Teach me your way, O Lord, and lead me on a level path because of my enemies.* "Path" was the word that shimmered. *Hmmmm, what was my path? What did that mean during this deadly disease?* The enemies were germs and cancer.

My particular cancer was lymphoma, a cancer of the lymph nodes in the body. Just as pink ribbons and all things pink signal breast cancer awareness, the color for lymphoma is lime green. It's not as well known. Probably no one knows this unless they have it, and I bet a lot of people who have it have no idea.

Earlier, I had painted a paper towel lime green, thinking I could use it as a backdrop somewhere. Now I positioned it and glued it into my big art journal. The word "path" was still shining in my head when suddenly, I began to see a yellow brick road weaving itself through the lymphoma. "Aha!" I thought to myself. "I am going to be like Dorothy in *The Wizard of Oz.* I will sing and dance my way through this disease!" I could hear Dorothy, the scarecrow, the lion, and the tin man singing in my head: *Follow the yellow brick road! Follow the yellow brick road! Follow, follow, follow, follow—follow the yellow brick road!*

I then began writing using the dominant/nondominant hands. Writing with the dominant hand, I asked, "Who are you?" The response came through the nondominant hand: *I am your path, your very own yellow brick road.*

"What is your message for me?" *I will not lead you astray. I will navigate you through this disease, and you will be victorious.*

"What do you need from me?" *Listen well. Trust the inner voice of love.*

I took this as a promise that God would not abandon me in this but would instead guide me clearly through this cancer experience.

I have heard lectures on the science of why this process of using the dominant and nondominant hand works. Dr. Roger Sperry won the Nobel Prize in 1981 for his pioneering research documenting the differences between the functions of the right and left brain in humans. Lucia Capacchione pioneered the use of the nondominant hand as a way to access the right brain and inner wisdom. I cannot remember everything I have read on his subject. I knew only that doing these exercises with the right and left hands calmed my worries and brought me peace. No, doing the exercise did not give me a flash of energy. I did not gain enormous insight into any problem.

What happened was that I quit beating myself up about my not–functioning–very–well life. I felt more compassion for me. The mental whips and ropes that I can use to lash out at myself when I don't think I am accomplishing enough were held at bay. I did not have to conquer the world. I did not have to dust my house or vacuum floors. I could just "be" and appreciate the gift of quiet.

Nothing changed on the outside of my life, but a shift occurred within me. I became far more peaceful, accepting and loving, not just of myself, but of others and the entire situation. Coping with the disease and its side effects became manageable.

INTEGRATIVE MEDICINE

By the end of October 2015, I was losing muscle tone. I could see it in my flabby arms that seemed to have become giant wings. I realized I could never go sleeveless again. I was losing strength. Opening a jar became nearly impossible.

It was time to take action. I met with the physical therapist over at MD Anderson who is a part of their integrative medicine department. It was time to exercise. She gave me lots of reasons why moving one's body is beneficial. "I know all these things," I told her. "I'm just too tired to do anything. My life right now is all about the living room couch."

I lay on a paper-covered table in a bright, fluorescent-lit examining room. I spoke to her from the table because sitting up in a chair was too exhausting. "I don't really mind the fatigue," I told her. "It's not so bad. As long as I am not nauseous or hurting anywhere, this cancer gig is doable."

She put me through some simple tests to see where I was physically. I only had trouble with one of them—being unable to stand and balance on my left foot for 60 seconds. I toppled right over. The therapist, whose name is Carol, left the room briefly. When she returned, she brought printouts showing nine different exercises. We did them together. None of them seemed difficult. One of them involved standing on one foot for as long as I could. Pat Clark, flamingo. I thought of the flamingo birds at the San Antonio zoo all standing around on one foot. I needed to get a pink shawl.

"Try walking every day," she said, "for just 5 minutes. You only must walk for 5 minutes—10 if you can do it. Don't think you have to be intimidated by long periods of exercise. We start gently. We go slowly. The important thing is to start doing SOMETHING." I did all those things with her, then came home and lay on the couch for the rest of the day.

In an effort to get healthy I availed, myself of nearly every service they offered at MD Anderson's integrative medicine department—things like oncology massage, acupuncture, counseling, and various kinds of meditation. Some of the things were offered in MD Anderson's main building. Others were offered in their newer building across the street.

I decided to try meditation. There was a time when I would not have been caught dead at a Tibetan Bon Meditation. Anything that did not line up with western Christianity was off limits in my book. The Bible doesn't say anything about Tibetan Bon Meditation. Well, the Bible doesn't say anything about a lot of things—like algebra or calculus. You don't go to the Bible to learn how to drive a car or to find a new recipe either.

Nowadays, if the teaching lines up with what I believe to be true, if I don't have to worship something weird, if it is gentle and promotes healing and wholeness, then I am generally in. There are all kinds of credible studies that show this meditation practice helps people heal when used with chemotherapy. That's why they offer it at MD Anderson. If it was mainstream for them, that was recommendation enough for me. I was willing to try virtually anything that might help.

We sat on meditation cushions covered with plastic since everything at MD Anderson is sanitized. The instructor introduced himself as an Argentinian who accompanied his father to MD Anderson as a caregiver years ago. He became fascinated with the wellness work underway there at the time. They offered him a faculty position, and he started offering classes every Tuesday morning.

The seven of us attendees, in various stages of cancer, sat in a loose circle—some of us in chairs and the others on the floor on the cushions that were spread out. "Focus on your breath," he told us. We closed our eyes and breathed in and out slowly. "Feel it in your chest. Now move it to your stomach." Then he led us in a guided journey where we paid attention to our breath the entire time. It was extraordinarily peaceful. It resembles what Christians call centering prayer, but the focus was on our breath instead of a sacred word whenever "monkey mind" took over. Monkey mind is that phenomenon that shows up when we begin to pray, and the mind becomes restless as it thinks of a thousand different things—what to cook for dinner, my to-do list, worries about my children.

Following the teacher's words made it much easier to stay in tune with the meditation than just sitting in silent prayer. After a while, he added another breathing technique and some movement. That was cool. I loved that part. It was energizing—enough for me to walk back to MD Anderson's main building over the sky bridge that links the two structures.

I made it to the other side and waited in the pouring rain for Forrest to come pick me up. Once home, I collapsed on the couch for the rest of the day. I needed to learn how to pace myself. Feeling great one day did not mean I could overdo it. I worried how I would ever make it to 10,000 steps on a Fitbit. It exhausted me even to think about it. The temptation to judge and criticize myself for years of neglect returned.

I was learning that it takes a lot of time and focus to be healthy with exercise, good nutrition, enough water, prayer, and meditation. This became a full-time job. I don't know how anyone can do it and hold down a job, much less a career that involves a lot of overtime. It had been too easy to put myself on the back burner. Work had always come first. I did not have much of a support team when it came to exercise, and I needed to find one. Old habits die hard, and frankly, I did not know whether I could do it.

Lying on the couch, looking through the glass window in my living room, I decided to give it a try. I would cling to the promise from Isaiah: *They that wait upon the Lord will renew their strength. They will mount up with wings as eagles. They will run and not be weary. They will walk and not faint.*

My prayer was simple: "Teach me, Lord. Teach me to wait upon you."

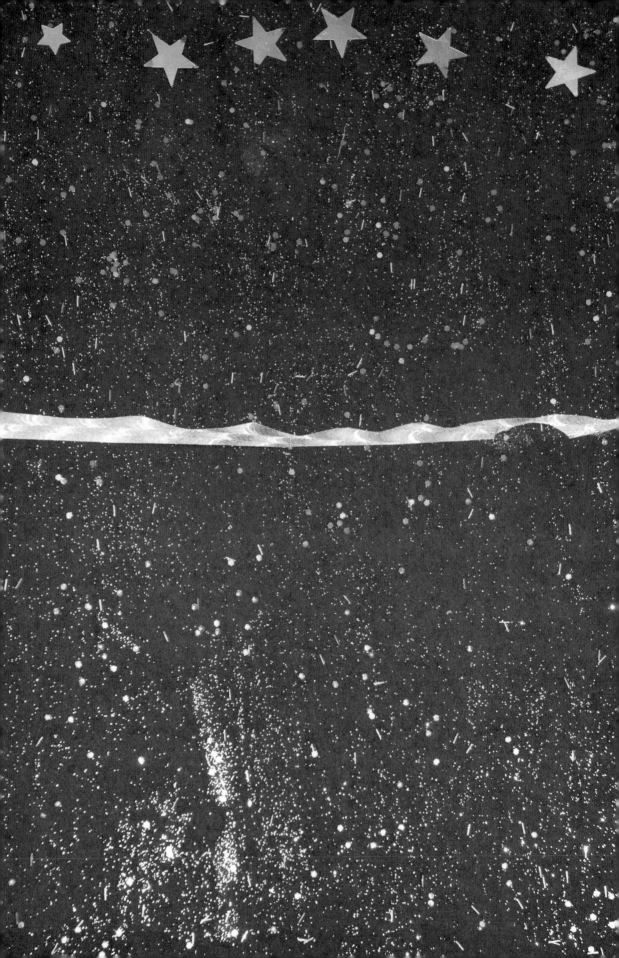

ALASKA

*Wait for the Lord, be strong, and let your heart take courage;
wait for the Lord!* (Psalm 27:14)

One summer day in July 2014, I stood in a roughly hewn cabin wondering how in the world anyone could live there year-round. It was probably 300 to 400 square feet. Heavy curtains covered the single window. An exposed light bulb provided the room's light. The place was Spartan with only the barest essentials like a bed in the corner, a table with two chairs, a small kitchenette, and some shelves that lined two of the walls. It was nearly 10 o'clock at night, but outside it looked as though it were 10 o'clock in the morning. This was Alaska in the wilderness, somewhere north of Coldspot, somewhere in the Arctic Circle in summer where the sun never sets. My sister, Dana, and I had come out of curiosity, catching a small flight out of Fairbanks for the evening's journey.

I have no idea what the man's name was who lived there, but we marveled at his stories. He told us of winter and temperatures that plunged to 60 degrees below zero. He told us how he trapped animals and spent all summer preparing for the long, dark winter that would follow. As he spoke, my eyes perused that cabin, wondering what a person would need to survive in that kind of climate.

It was an ugly cabin with no decorative touches—just rough, dark wooden walls and a ceiling made from the same kind of wood. There were hazy Mason jars filled with screws and nuts and bolts. A shelf that lined one wall held some flour and sugar. There was a coffee pot and a table where paper was stacked as though he had been writing. He told us there was Wi-Fi, but very, very slow. Even in Alaska, in one of the most remote parts of the earth, he could still get

Wi-Fi, still keep in touch. It was amazing to me! I did not see a toilet, and I do not remember running water. I should have asked, but I did not. What an experience to use an outhouse in 60 degrees below zero temperatures!

Outside, I had noticed a garden growing. He was growing cabbages, carrots, cucumbers, and beets. I don't remember what else. Because there is constant daylight in summer, plants flourish in Alaska, even out there. Not only that, it wasn't that cold. A windbreaker was all we needed. It was the end of July, and we swatted giant mosquitoes. I thought they were bad in Texas. Hah! Alaska mosquitoes are big and vicious. I was surprised.

The pioneer showed us his winter coat lined with animal fur that appeared to be 4 to 6 inches thick. So that's how they do it! That's how they endure the extreme cold. The coat was almost too heavy to lift. As he spoke, my mind checked out—it often does when I am on information overload. What I remember thinking is that I could never live like that. We were having enough trouble adjusting to the bright light of endless day. We could barely fathom what it would be like to live with never-ending night, even if we could regularly see the northern lights streaking across the darkened sky.

I think now of all the questions I should have asked him, things I have thought about since we were there. What about clean clothes and toileting and other things that use water? What did he do in the long winters? What kind of community did he have with the other nearby cabins? There were not enough to form a town, but still—what did they do? Were there children there? What about illness and seeing a doctor?

He spoke of his wife and their life together, although we did not get to meet her. "The high point of the year for her," he said, "is when the streak of a yellow sunrise cuts through the darkness, and we know for sure that spring will come. She watches for it, and she waits."

I imagined her waiting through the long night of a frozen Alaskan winter, living in an ugly one-room cabin, and watching for the first sign of spring that would signal for them that this present darkness would not last forever. As he spoke of his beloved and her waiting, I could feel hope begin to rise within me too.

Right then I thought, "This is the clearest picture I have ever seen of what it means to wait on the Lord." That phrase, "wait for the Lord," is sprinkled throughout Scripture and is the last verse to my now beloved Psalm 27—the Psalm that guided me through the early days of this cancer experience: *Wait for the Lord, be strong, and let your heart take courage; wait for the Lord!*

Just as that Alaskan housewife waited through the darkness of a long winter to see the thin light of sunrise, so did I wait to see evidence that the sun would rise, that this cancer was being healed, and that I would once again thrive outdoors in the daylight. As surely as the dawn breaks through the darkened sky and signals spring, I sensed that my healing was also on the way. Spring and the time of recovery would come.

Too often I have equated hope with wishes. I hope I make a good grade on this test. I hope it doesn't rain for my party. I hope Forrest remembers to pick up our prescriptions on the way home from work. I don't think any of those things are hope anymore. For me, hope is that knowing, deep within, that ultimately things will work out. When things seem to be falling apart, when life is confined to a small space like that ugly cabin, hope is knowing that God is at work and will bring all things to conclusion in the end. It is also knowing that whatever hardship is underway will be used for good.

Waiting for the Lord is just that kind of hope, the hope the Alaskan housewife had in waiting for spring. She waited, knowing the sun would come. Now as I remembered that streak of light, I thought of other signs of hope that came my way.

The Celts taught me that nature is the big book, and Scripture is the little book. John Calvin calls Scripture the spectacles that make everything else clear. In the season of healing, when my focus was off, and I was unable to concentrate on very little for any length of time, I would have to use the visual book of God's creation to help with the healing of my broken spirit. As I spent the days lying on my brown couch in the living room and watching the world through the glass panes of the window, nature spoke to me and gave me hope.

It was fall in Houston, and the trees outside would soon lose their leaves, letting them go in various ways. Some would drop them with a great flourish. Some would lose them to an overnight storm, and some like the pecan tree out front would hold on until everyone else had a turn before letting go of theirs. I was gradually letting go of this disease and felt a solidarity with them as I did with that Alaskan housewife whom I never met. Together we would all wait for the first signs of spring.

COMMUNION OF THE SAINTS

By now it was November 1, the first Sunday of November, the eve before my third chemotherapy. I found myself in a funk. It could have been the weather or trying to do too much or the chemotherapy buildup in my body. Who knew? I was more exhausted than I had ever been. I felt limp, on the inside and on the outside, like one of those soft brown and wet fall leaves that had landed on my doorstep.

My prayer life sucked, to put it bluntly. This was painful to admit as a Minister of the Word and Sacrament. We are supposed to be praying always, without ceasing according to the Bible. I was known in some circles as a prayer warrior or the spiritual one, but Lord, those days I was doing my best just to mouth the words, *Help* or *Thank you.* People were always saying to me something like, "Oh, you have a direct line. Would you pray for... "Fill in the blank." I would say, "Yes, of course," but usually I could only call the person's name with the simplest of requests. Frankly, there had not been much cloth in me to put on that skeleton of prayer.

November 1, 2015, was different. I missed attending church and went looking online for something that might help me spiritually. There, I spotted an e-mail from an Episcopal priest named Barbara Crofton who lives somewhere on the East Coast. She invited her readers to pray with her and suggested a website, www.missiononstclare.com, to help us do that. That particular website features a morning prayer service in the Episcopal tradition every day.

That sounded like a good idea considering my sorry state. I clicked on the link. It led me to the site for morning prayer. There, I read all the Scriptures for the day and prayed the prayers that others had written centuries ago. When I came to the Litany for All Saints Day, I stopped, holding my breath. They were praying to all those ancient and modern saints as though they were still alive.

Scripture teaches us that we are surrounded by a great cloud of witnesses (Hebrews 12:1) who are very much alive, but I had never thought much about contacting them. I mean I am a Protestant after all. Our ancestors were horrified by statues of saints and prayers to them. They ripped them out or shattered them. We go directly to God when we pray. We don't ask anyone who has died to intercede for us. This felt a little weird to me, quite frankly, but I decided to go ahead with the liturgy.

The prayers on the website for the Sunday of the Communion of Saints began with Abraham and Sarah, who are the founding patriarch and matriarch of Judaism and Christianity (Abraham is also the patriarch of Islam). The process of praying the prayer was simple: *Abraham and Sarah, Stand beside us!* I pictured them in my mind's eye, thought of all the hardships they had endured, and because I was in such bad shape this season plus praying alone, I modified the phrase to be, Abraham and Sarah, *Stand beside me!*

The liturgy moved through all the patriarchs—*Isaac and Rebecca, Jacob and Rachel and Leah, makers of the covenant...Stand beside me!* The great Bible heroes were all there, and I remembered each one: Moses, David, Mary, Mary Magdalene, John the Baptizer. I saw them, called their names out loud, and prayed, *Stand beside me!*

Many of the great heroes and heroines of the faith were named in the litany —all the regulars but also people like Julian of Norwich and Hildegard of Bingen, Bach and Mozart, Dorothy Day, Oscar Romero and Martin Luther King. I pictured them all in my mind, said their names, and prayed along with the liturgy, *Stand beside me!*

Slowly, slowly, that great cloud of people began to form in my consciousness. I thought of their terrible struggles and the difficult times they had endured. In my mind they surrounded me, then stood beside me, stretching out as far as my eyes could see. I remembered those whose lives had touched me personally and began to call to them: *Mama and Daddy, stand by me. Grandma Schuck and Grandma Persch, stand by me. Uncle Ernie, stand by me.* You get the picture. I prayed repeatedly and named everyone in my family who had passed on to another life.

From there, I moved on to all the sweet people, and some of them stubborn, whose funerals I officiated. Oh, I have loved some of them more than I could say. I thought of deceased church members, called their names, and as I called the names, they came forward and surrounded me.

When I finished the litany, I clicked on the button to hear the choir sing the hymn, "For All the Saints." I sang, as best I could, all the verses with them. I especially loved the second verse: *Thou wast their rock, their fortress, and their might; Thou, Lord, their captain in the well-fought fight; thou in the darkness drear, their one true Light, Alleluia! Alleluia!*

By then tears had filled my eyes and flowed down my cheeks, not from sadness, but from seeing all those blessed people surrounding me and standing by me during this painful season of my life. I wept because I am part of a long line of faithful people whose ministries go back thousands of years. I wept because I felt incredibly strengthened by their presence during this current cancer ordeal and honored to be a part of their company. I wept even as I wrote this because the images remain so powerful.

I will never forget them or the warmth that surrounded me as they came forward to stand beside me. Truly, I felt buoyed and uplifted, strengthened on the inside in a way I do not ever remember. What a powerful, powerful, emotional experience!

Here's the bottom line. I was ready to face chemotherapy again the next day.

I could do this.

BUTTERFLIES

It shimmered.

It beckoned me.

It refused to let me go.

As I gazed upon it, I felt a shift within me – the very presence of God I think. Something stirred within me in a powerful way. Suddenly I sensed a future opening that was lovely and beautiful, joyful, soulful and sparkly. It was my very first glimpse of a life without cancer, and it almost took my breath away.

It was a pile of Monarch butterflies gracing the November 2015 cover of the Austin Seminary faculty journal. It fell through the mail chute of my front door. Right away I made it my cover photo on Facebook. I was a little fearful of talking to it though.

Afraid of what, Pat?

Joy?

Go figure!

Early the next morning before sunrise I pulled up some courage and asked the questions: Who are you? *I am your new life. I am joy. I am full and abundant. I am the Scripture you have always loved from the gospel of John: "I came that they might have life and have it abundantly."*

So, what is your message to me? *Don't be afraid. You have always made life harder than it has to be. You have lived with so much angst and tension and stress. You never understood the resources you had within you. It's time to let all of that go and allow joy and lightheartedness to be your guide.*

What do you need from me? *Pay attention! Time on task during your healing time. You will make it through this. Chin up! Forward!*

The afternoon before, my wonderful nurse friend, Susie, came for a visit. I was still in my pajamas and talked to her while reclining on the couch.

"Do you think the treatment is working?" she asked me. Hmmmm. How would I answer that? It's a hard question since I did not have many symptoms of this disease. I never felt a tumor before diagnosis. I did not feel any that day. It simply presented itself as stage 4 cancer without all the usual fanfare. I "glistened" for a couple of weeks before I started treatment, and I did not do that anymore. I was sleeping better.

The month before my diagnosis, I marveled that I seemed to be able to eat a lot of food without seeing the pounds show up. Now I seemed to be packing it on. Despite the bouts of fatigue, my energy level seemed a little better. Other than that, I did not have any hard scientific evidence. No test results. All I had was this little picture of butterflies. I felt silly bringing that up. I mean my butterfly picture would not hold up in court, would it? What if it wasn't true? What if I was making a fool of myself? What if?

I resembled Gideon, a puny little guy in the Bible whom God called to conquer the Midianites. He was nervous about it. After all, he was not the sort one pictures when one thinks about a warrior with all the accompanying blood and guts. He kept asking God for signs. God gave them. It pissed off all the enemies, they started rattling their swords, and Gideon pleaded again: "Look," he said, "I am going to just place a piece of wool here on the floor. If there is dew on the fleece but everything else is dry, then I will believe you're going to save Israel through me." It happened. Gideon was still nervous and said, "OK, this time make the ground dry and the fleece soaking wet." Sure enough, that happened too, just like he asked. Gideon then felt empowered and went on to defeat the Midianites.

So, what about me and the butterflies? Like Gideon, I needed some confirmation that this was coming from God and not my imagination. A sign would have been nice—a PET scan maybe or something like that.

What I believe God gave me was this: I was out at the farm the next week with my husband. It was one of those beautiful fall days when the air is just starting to turn cooler. I sat on a sawed-off tree stump in my blue jeans. It had a flat, smooth surface and was nearly chair height. I was wearing my gray fleece jacket and sat with my right leg on the ground. My left ankle rested on my right knee. I was enjoying the sun and the bright blue sky when a Monarch butterfly landed on my ankle. It stayed there about 15 minutes.

I sat very still all the while it was there. As it sat there opening and closing its wings, I took it as my personal sign from God that I would survive this chemotherapy and live without cancer. I felt warmed in my heart.

I talked to Max about the butterflies. He's my guru—counselor, writing coach, great encourager, spiritual guide, creator of fun and fabulous imagery. A conversation with Max is a little like sitting with a fire hose on full blast. I try to take notes, but his responses come so fast it's hard to take it all in. I told him I had this shimmery image of butterflies for my future and asked him what he thought about it. As best I can remember, he said something like, "We walk differently if we know we're walking towards the sun. Once we have felt the future, every day will be shaped. Whatever comes, comes."

I think that's true. Whether the butterflies meant life without cancer for me or whether they were the promise of resurrection in the afterlife, I cannot say. I decided right then, that very morning, that it did not really matter. The vision before me, either way, was joy, and that made all the difference.

THE NIGHTMARE

I dream every night. Usually my dreams are vivid, action-packed, on-the-move kind of happenings. I try to organize everybody into something, then tie up loose ends everywhere in the process, like a juggler tossing too many plates in the air.

But one night in November 2015, I had a different kind of dream. It was a doozie! Its memory lingered, long after I awakened. I was more terrified than I have ever been. This was no gentle anxiety. Raw, intense, primal fear gripped me like nothing I can remember. Chills ran up and down my body. The hair on my arms stood straight up. I shrank on the inside. It felt endless even though it must have lasted only a minute or less.

In the dream, I stood at the edge of a precipice looking into a large, black hole that threatened to envelop me. I was scared and paralyzed, unable to move.

I could only stare into the terrifying darkness. I awakened with a start. "It's just a dream," I told myself and tried to shake it off, but its memory lingered.

When a dream presents itself with that kind of force, it needs to be dealt with. Any situation in life that causes that kind of strong emotion is a message to stop and pay attention. Here is the problem I faced that morning: Even though this was just a dream, I could not focus on it. I was afraid to invite it to tell its story. It was still too powerful. I went downstairs and poured myself a cup of coffee. I put an ice cube in it as I usually do, then went to the comfortable chair in the living room. As I drank, my mind wandered. I noticed the dust particles in the air. I looked at my stack of magazines on the coffee table. I thought about the things I needed to do and looked around for a pad of paper so that I could make a list. I was stalling. I knew I needed to address the dream. "Help!" I prayed. That was my standard prayer when I was on overwhelm.

When I finally drummed up enough courage, I pulled out my journal and colored a big, black hole. Then I began to talk to it one on one, through my writing, alternating between the dominant and nondominant hands. Feelings are feelings. They come, and they go. It's when we do not allow them a voice and deal with them that we get into trouble. Or at least that's when I get into trouble. I am excellent at stuffing feelings, but on this day, I decided to deal with them.

It was not easy. I could almost hear a sinister Halloween-type voice gloating in triumph as I scribbled the black hole larger and larger. It was, after all, a giant fear. Through the nondominant hand, the black hole told me that its name was fear of annihilation, that its entire way of being and living was now threatened. This was not a little lack of courage in facing it; this was gargantuan in its scope.

I remembered, finally, that Scripture teaches the antidote to fear—love. In my mind's eye, I gently invited the big, black hole to sit on my lap. It consented to do just that, and so we sat there in my mind for a few minutes, with me trying to hold the black hole that was almost smothering me. As I held the fear in my body, I tried as best I could to surround it with love and not to judge myself for being silly. We sat, just the two of us, fear and me, in the red chair in my living room, in the quiet. All the while I tried to surround it with love.

What happened next, I would never have predicted. The big, scary, black hole shrank to a tiny little speck. No more fear. No more monster. No more threat of annihilation. No big deal. All the fear vanished in a flash. I was at peace. I could get on with the business of the day, my life.

Why does it take so long to remember the simple tools for healing? Why is my first response to give into fear and trembling rather than remembering I am not powerless? When I sit with scary feelings and surround them with love, they always, always disappear. Love is stronger than any feeling of fear. I felt engulfed by the love of God who has promised never to let me or anyone else go.

I was sure that darkness would try to have its way with me again, perhaps many times as I wandered through the treatment of this disease. What I was learning from cancer, whether it ultimately killed me or not, is that it is possible to live with serenity and love in the face of it. No terror on earth is a match for love. I began to feel whole and complete, confident even. I was not so naive as to think that scary feelings and things will never surface again. Of course, they would! What I needed to remember was to recognize them for what they are—feelings that can leave as easily as they come. To deal with them with love would be the challenge.

THE COCOON

Hide me in the shadow of your wings. (Psalm 17:8)

*T*he precautions continued. I had just finished my third chemotherapy 6 days earlier. Before sunrise, the possibility that I could feel well, not just good, but really, really good dawned on me. I began to imagine my life with energy, without the crippling fatigue that has dogged me for most of my life. My low energy level has always been my great secret, a fact of life that has hampered me ever since I can remember.

When I was a little girl, I had severe asthma. It was so bad that I almost died from it, or so they told me. What I remember from the illness is the doctor's clear instruction to me: "You must not exercise, not now, not ever. You must not get winded. It could kill you." I have not had an asthma attack for more than 50 years, and yet, and yet, I still hear that doctor's voice in my head: "Don't get winded. Don't sweat. You could bring on an attack. You could die!"

Because of his advice, I have lived a sedentary life. One of my earliest report cards says, "Patty is excellent in her seat work." Do I ever know how to sit! Ministry is all about sitting—through endless meetings, study and writing, and sitting and listening to people. I sit very well! The downside is that I have rarely had the stamina to function an entire day. Either I would find a way to sneak a nap in the daytime, or I would come home and lie on the couch, unable to marshal enough energy to do anything.

If you were to ask my children about their memories of me, they would probably talk about my lying on the couch—a lot of lying on the couch. I never had much energy to get up and go because I never exercised. I loaded us up with carbohydrates. How much different my life would have been if I had known early on that I had a gluten intolerance and that a little exercise would not kill me!

In church I always sampled the concoctions that the women of the church brought to covered-dish dinners. I never wanted to hurt anyone's feelings by refusing their food. I was too tired to exercise, and then there was always the inner voice that warned, "It could kill you."

On this warm November morning, I found myself held in a sort of cocoon, a safe place, hidden away from the world. I rarely, if ever, went out in public. People who visited me had to wear masks sometimes and always wash their hands. I lived in a sterile environment that was overkill in hindsight, but the danger of infection was great for someone with lymphoma. We were taking precautions. My food was delivered fresh every morning, and it was all healthy—no sugar, no flour of any kind or gluten, and perfectly balanced. We did not eat out.

In my little cocoon, there was time to think and to begin to imagine what my life would look like without cancer. What if I put aside the notion that things are bad, and they can only get worse? What if I could believe that God has a wonderful future for me? What if my new life could be full of energy without the thought patterns that had dragged me down?

I began to feel gratitude for such a dedicated time to heal. Now I had the blessing of time to journal and make sense of what was going on with me. My art mentor, Lucia Capacchione, has always said, "Illness is the great teacher." Boy is that ever true! There was nothing like being stopped in my tracks to make me sit up and take notice.

Time for kindergarten art. This cocoon idea was growing. Forrest and I had made a quick early morning trip to the art supply store, where I bought some textured papers. I chose a chocolate brown paper for a giant tree trunk, then illustrated the cocoon with green paper. That to me showed growth. I believed I was growing healthier. I looked at it for a while, then began a conversation with that cocoon. I asked questions with my dominant hand and answered with the nondominant hand.

I wrote the first question with my right, dominant hand, "Little green cocoon, who are you and why are you here?" She answered through the nondominant hand; *I am your healing place. I am here held safely in the great arms of God. I am your sanctuary, your place of refuge. I am protecting you while you undergo the process of transformation.*

Switching back to the dominant hand, I wrote, "What is your message to me?" *This is all about healing years of neglect. This is about becoming whole. Your temptation is to cut this process too short—to go running around willy-nilly doing whatever you want and not necessarily listening to my voice. Everything else becomes a priority for you. You must ask daily what my priority is for you, and then you must find the courage to do that instead of giving in to what you think everyone else wants you to do. Cancer is your wake-up call. This is the time you will discover what your ministry really is for the rest of your life on earth.*

"What do you need from me?" *Focus. Commitment to the Lucia work, the morning prayer, simple exercising until you are strong, but those will become your daily spiritual disciplines forever. Pay attention to my voice, to the signs that are all around you—like the butterfly picture you found on the seminary journal cover. You will indeed thrive. You are thriving now in this cocoon. It gets better. Do not be afraid!*

I have often wondered whether these words of wisdom come from my own ego-centered nature. Is this just wishful thinking or does it come from some deep place within me where the Holy Spirit resides? I have learned to ask more questions about these nondominant hand insights, although I seldom write these out. I will ask myself things like, *If I believe this or do this, does it help me to become more loving or more whole? Does it put me on the side of truth and justice? Does it line up to be true with the central teachings of Scripture? Are the fruits of the Spirit (love, joy, peace, patience, kindness, generosity, faithfulness, gentleness, and self-control) evident if I take this path?*

In seminary, the Quakers taught me the importance of listening for the inner voice as one of the primary ways God leads us. What I have had to admit to myself is that I don't always want to listen or to be led. I am a rebel at heart, always have been. I don't like anyone, even God, telling me what to do. I don't like giving up control.

Now I sensed once again that my back was up against the wall, so to speak. I was being led by this inner voice of love, and quite frankly, following this was life-giving. I was reminded of Jesus' famous words that begin the ancient sacrament of communion: *Take my yoke upon you and learn from me for I am gentle and humble in heart, and you will find rest for your soul.*

There sitting in my cocoon in the early morning light and pondering all these things, I took a step. I surrendered my life to God again. The first time I did that was with wails and tears. I did not realize how quickly I would change my mind. This time was quieter. It was an acceptance, a yielding. I felt trust opening within me, and the assurance that everything would be fine. I vowed again to take one step, one day at a time.

Nov. 10, 2015 How do I feel right now?

LITTLE PATTY

I will praise you for I am fearfully and wonderfully made.
(Psalm 139)

I held her in my arms, and surprisingly, my eyes filled with tears. One by one we passed the plastic, blanket-wrapped doll to one another in the circle. The doll represented our inner child. I do not remember the name of the workshop or who presented it. It was summer 1989 at the Presbyterian conference center in Montreat, North Carolina. The gracious women of my church had funded my trip to the annual women's conference before I was installed as their new president.

I passed the life-sized baby doll in her pastel blanket to the woman seated beside me, as the speaker talked about feelings, the importance of honoring them, and the little child who lives within each of us. Years later, I would discover one of Lucia Capacchione's books, *Recovering Your Inner Child*. That book set me on the meandering path where I found myself that morning.

I named my inner child "Little Patty." How quick I am to ignore her! I try to figure everything out intellectually and fail to tap into soul-generated inner wisdom. It's also easy to give into all manner of distractions. On that day, November 10, 2015, Little Patty told me off in my journal in no uncertain terms. I drew her picture with simple black lines, and through my nondominant hand, she began to speak with great sadness and pointed remarks.

She told me she was weary of having me judge her all the time. As she raised her arms in praise to a life-giving Scripture, she seemed tentative and hesitant. Look how tentative she was when she raised her arms in praise to a verse from Psalm 139:14 *I will praise you for I am fearfully and wonderfully made.* Patty was very hesitant—terrified even. The poor child was afraid of getting pummeled!

I longed to pick her off the page and cradle her in my arms as I did that plastic baby in a blanket so many years ago at Montreat. Right then, when I looked at the picture, I knew why I had lymphoma, the cancer of the defense system, and not some other kind of cancer. Little Patty simply could not take getting blasted any more. She had lost all her defenses and lay terrified, unable to brace herself from the next onslaught of judgment.

I thought of all the times I had given into judging myself. My mantra could easily be "not good enough." I could find the flaw in everything. I was a news reporter after all. I knew how to ask hard questions and find the chink in someone's armor, then poke around there. I could be merciless. Seminary mirrored that—find the flaw and run with it. The more I engaged in critical thought, the easier it became. Negativity and complaining had become my way of life.

Now I thought about that poor, defenseless inner child. How many times I have judged myself! Every sermon was agony in fighting off the inner critic. Forrest grew weary of listening to me all the way to church on Sunday mornings when I would say, "This is a piece of crap! This is shit! What am I going to do? I can't get up there and give this sermon!"

He would tell me not to trash it, saying it was really good. "Stop being so negative," he would caution me. "It is the gift God has given you, and you are not the judge."

I judged myself in every way—as an inferior wife, an inferior mother, an inferior housekeeper, you name it. I never felt good enough. I could blame my childhood and lack of a support system. My parents died young, but the negative, mean voice of my stepfather stayed within me long after we parted ways. On my own, I had internalized his voice, and now that voice had pummeled Little Patty almost to death. She was too weary to fight the incoming blasts any more.

That harsh voice kept my creativity at bay. I would get an idea of something to write, then tear it up after I had judged it. When I offered something handmade, it came with an apology. I downplayed compliments. O my, when I thought about it, the list was endless!

I complain and feel sad about the meanness of American society these days. We get offended by anything and everything. We judge and criticize, sort and come up with labels. Here's where it starts. It begins within me when I destroy in my mind every creative thought that wants to be birthed. It begins with me every single time that I fail to begin something because I am fearful that what I write or draw or cut or paste will not be perfect. It begins with me whenever I give into judgment and fail to love myself and the child who lives within me.

If I cannot learn to love vulnerable Little Patty, how can I possibly love anyone else? I can jump quickly, in the twinkling of an eye, to knee jerk criticism! Somehow, I realized that my healing from cancer was all about allowing this little precious, young girl to feel loved, and loved unconditionally, instead of facing harsh criticism every time she makes a move. My inner healing began that morning with Little Patty raising her arms as she listened to the Psalm that brought her life. That tentative stance would never move to confidence without my surrounding her with love. From there it could grow.

Jesus said, *Unless you become as a little child, you will never enter the kingdom of heaven.* Somehow getting in touch with this long ignored and forgotten child, listening to her, even delighting in her, and loving her would be the key to my healing and eventual thriving. This was where the rubber met the road. I knew these things but had a habit of forgetting. I get distracted by life.

In some ways, in a lot of ways, I regretted beginning my online journal. Yes, it had been wonderful to see hearts and read comments. It made me feel less isolated, homebound as I was. Here was the new issue that showed up with the art I drew that day. I was in effect inviting others into the painful parts of my life where I did not have it all worked out. It was scary. It was fresh. It was raw on the inside and primitive. There was shame involved. It was not like me to be that vulnerable when I did not have it all organized and sanitized and tied up with a pretty bow.

I could share my struggles easily after I had already worked through everything. Then I could sound all wise about it, detached even, as though I was describing something that happened in my distant past and was no longer holding me captive. This fear of being vulnerable whispered to me that it was the next layer to be discarded. I crossed a threshold. I wondered if the writing would end that day with this piece. I didn't know. What I knew for sure is that the next time someone complimented my kindergarten art, I would say thank you instead of talking about how silly and stupid it is. That's where I would begin.

THE FARM

We sat in the shelter of two enormous oak trees. In the quiet of a gentle afternoon in 1976, peace descended upon us, my mother-in-law and me. It was a different kind of peace than I had known. I sensed the very presence of God in those trees. In this moment we knew our long search for land was over and ended outside Shiner, Texas. This was our farm, our home, our sanctuary and refuge. Shortly thereafter Forrest and I and his parents bought it with his sisters and the help of the GI bill, and I consecrated it to God as a place of peace and sanctuary.

In the early days, there was only one little wooden house without plumbing and a few sheds that once held turkeys. We used an outhouse, never popular with the girls in the family. We hand-pumped water from a well, then heated it on the electric stove for cooking, cleaning, and bathing on Saturday nights in the smokehouse. We marveled that the sweet Czech couple who had lived there for 44 years never enjoyed indoor plumbing.

After Forrest's parents died, we took the money they had passed on and moved a small wooden three-bedroom home to the farm. My husband dreamed of a central gathering place that would keep his family together, maintaining the closeness they had enjoyed when his parents were alive. The family set about expanding and remodeling it. We added a second story and built wings on the sides. Forrest and I and his sisters each had a bedroom on the ground floor. Among us we had six children, and we built six bedrooms, a bathroom, and a gathering area on the upper floor.

For years, we spent every weekend at the farm wiring, plumbing, nailing sheetrock, putting down floors, and painting. We had a hot tub before we had indoor plumbing. The process of building helped us move through our grief and bond as an extended family. My husband's dream came true. Later we added a large porch when our nephew and his bride wanted to be married at the farm and needed a dance floor. Forrest and his brother-in-law built a labyrinth in a grove of oak trees, a sacred place to me. Finally, we added another huge porch because we enjoyed the first one so much.

We have been going to the farm for more than 40 years now, and with time have come tons of memories—late nights out by the campfire, Thanksgivings and delicious food, and long walks through the 67 acres of wooded area, although nowadays we usually ride the golf carts. We have hosted many retreats for church groups, clergy needing a respite after Holy Week and Easter, art groups, and even a writers' group. Spring Branch Presbyterian Church gave us a cow and her calf as a farewell gift after my tenure there. That generous gift started our small herd. Ah, yes, wonderful, wonderful memories!

Only after we bought the farm did I realize how disconnected I was from the land. Always a city girl, I lived on concrete streets with neighbors only a few feet away. Country life was completely foreign to me. It is radically different. For one thing, it's quiet. It's dark at night, really dark. We can see the stars. Some nights are breathtaking! All of this glory helps me put my life in perspective and connects me to something much larger than myself.

At night, walking the labyrinth by torch light, or sitting around the campfire, bathed by the warmth of the fire, my spirit draws upward, and I recall the words of Psalm 8: *When I consider your heavens, the work of your fingers, the moon and the stars, which you have set in place, what is man that you are mindful of him....*

How unlike the world at MD Anderson Cancer Center! The buildings of that facility are massive, boxed shapes and functional with traffic snarled around them. The waiting rooms in the lymphoma clinic are noisy and bustling, not just with the continual barking of names, but also from wall-mounted televisions. A single technician will check the vital signs of 100 patients a day. The chemotherapy treatment areas run behind constantly, and patients who are ill lie on couches, waiting to hear their name called before they can receive their prescribed infusion. Lunch lines are long but move efficiently. There are people everywhere!

The waiting rooms are small and sterile. Because it is a teaching hospital, every office visit with a doctor includes several students, all wearing white coats. Computer printouts show exactly how body parts and functions are reacting to chemotherapy. Massive machines take PET scans and CT scans. Attendants wear blue latex gloves when they touch you. The world of illness and treatment is full of non-natural spaces.

Unlike MD Anderson, our Shiner farm grounds me. I look at those old oaks that have stood for hundreds, maybe thousands of years, and feel their strength. How many storms they have withstood! How many droughts! One year we heard a massive, thunderous sound in the early morning hours as we slept. When we investigated, we noticed one of the sprawling arms of our favorite oak tree lying on the ground. Now instead of two giant arms, it has only one. It's a broken tree now, yet it stands, opening its one remaining arm to give shelter and solace to anyone.

The broken tree has become the symbol for the farm, a place of healing and respite. The tree functions beautifully despite its giant wound. No words are needed to prove its point. This one-armed tree stands tall as a model of courage and the ability to function despite a significant setback.

One afternoon, during treatment I sat quietly in the shadow of the broken oak tree. I saw the pretty sky. I heard the cardinals singing. I felt the grass under my feet. I rocked gently in a white wrought-iron chair and felt the cool breeze on my face. After a while, I sensed that majestic tree saying to me, "Let my strength embrace you during this healing time. You will live. You will thrive. Listen. Deeply. Listen."

One blessing of cancer's great fatigue in my body is that I learned to find quiet in my soul. I was learning to be a human being instead of a human "doing."

I did not know if my energy would ever return. If it did not, I would be ok. I was learning to be still and listen, never more than when I came to the farm and spent time outdoors. My faith grew deeper within me because of it. Again, I felt the shift. I came to peace.

PATTY PERSCH
EL PASO
SAN ANTONIO MEXICO
UNIVERSITY of TEXAS
MARRIAGE to FORREST
germany
TREVOR
Eri
FARM
St. Andrew's
HQST-APTS
KTRH
ordination
St. Stephen
extended family friends
Presbytery Lucia
HEALING FROM CANCER

THE BOOK OF LIFE

All the days ordained for me were written in your book
before one of them came to be. (Psalm 139:16)

I felt nervous the day I awaited the results of my psychological exam before I was ordained to ministry. I had mailed in paperwork that had taken 12 hours to complete followed by two full days of testing. In 1994 Presbyterians required extensive testing before one could be ordained. Maybe they still do. After all, no one wants a fool for a minister or someone who could wreck a congregation.

I had taken test after test, and now it was time to hear the results. I had never been to a psychotherapist. If the counselor had said, "You are bat shit crazy!" I would have believed him or her and signed up for therapy. Instead he said, "You are very healthy." I felt an incredible sense of relief!

That long-ago conversation surfaced the night of November 8, 2015. It was the evening before I was to get the results of my PET scan. This one test would show whether or not the chemo was working. I sat down at the end of my kitchen island to do kindergarten art for Psalm 139:16: *All the days ordained for me were written in your book before one of them came to be.* This concept of the "Book of Life" had been on my mind for a while, ever since my Jewish friends prayed for me on the holy day of Yom Kippur, asking God that my name be included in the Book of Life for another year. I leafed through my art supplies and set to work. First, I cut out and pasted the image of an open book onto the page. I titled that page with my childhood name, Patty Persch.

I began to think about the key events in my life. Listing them, I started with El Paso, the city of my birth. Then there was the move to San Antonio and the summer I spent attending Mexico City College in Mexico City. I wrote down the University of Texas where I earned my first degree, my marriage to Forrest, and our time in Germany when he was an Army lieutenant. I drew in stick figures of our two children, Trevor and Emi. I added St. Andrew's Presbyterian Church in Houston where my faith was born and nurtured. Then came the Houston Graduate School of Theology and Austin Presbyterian Theological Seminary where I received masters' degrees.

Tears filled my eyes as I worked. Memories of my news career at KTRH flooded my consciousness, and I added that to the top of the second page, followed by ordination to ministry and the eight churches I had served. I included St. Stephen, which named me their pastor emerita. Presbytery, a regional governing body for the Gulf Coast, came next. I had served there for many years, including a stint as moderator (comparable to a president or a bishop for a one-year term). Finally, I included my training with art therapist Lucia Capacchione.

I paused. My eyes were wet. "What comes next?" I queried.

The answer floated into my mind: "Healing from Cancer." With more tears streaming down my face, I added those three words to my book of life. As I looked at my life on this page, I confidently left an open space. My life was neither finished nor going downhill! I left plenty of room to write more things later.

The experience was powerful. I wept more as I sat there on a bar stool at the island in my kitchen and stared at the page I had created.

A doctor's appointment the next day would give me the results of the scan. If the chemo was working, I would have my next treatment. Forrest, Trevor, and Emi would all go into that closet of a room with me. I felt buoyed by their presence, love, and support. God would also be in there with us, fulfilling the great promise of Scripture: *I am with you always, even to the end of the age.*

Chin up! Confident! I was ready to greet the next day.

After the appointment, my daughter, Emi Clark, wrote about the results from MD Anderson:

Yesterday we received big news. BIG NEWS. My brother Trevor, Dad and I all followed Mom into the little exam room and waited for the results of her first PET scan halfway through treatment.... Her doctor is clearly a very talented man and is doing an amazing job, but his bedside manner...well...he's a bit quiet and unemotional. He's got a very bland affect. So, when he came in and saw all of us there, he remarked that it was good we were there because, 'Good news it's gone,' delivered with no flourish. He might as well have said, 'I had a baked potato for lunch.' All of us were perplexed. Incredulously Mom asks, 'What?'

The cancer. It's gone. You can see right here. (He shows us impressive before and after pictures.) He says this as though he couldn't believe we had no idea what he was talking about. He sees this all the time. That's why he's so good, that's why MD Anderson is the best, that's why the BIG news was a bit of a non-event for him. But it was a HUGE event for us. We remained calm. Stunned. We asked questions then. What does this mean? What's next? I can't remember all he said exactly except that she had to finish her treatment by completing the last three rounds of chemo.

My mother clung with hope in anticipation of the answer to her most important question, about being cloistered in her home, not able to go out without great risk. 'Oh no,' he says, 'you shouldn't be punished. Take precautions and go live a normal life.' Mom says excitedly, 'I can go to the movies?' He holds up his hand, 'Well....' He's not so sure about that. So, we've been wondering what a 'normal life' looks like if public places are still discouraged.

We sat in the waiting room as we waited for chemotherapy and shared the good news via Facebook and texts. We read responses, shares, and numbers of 'likes.' Facebook is a great place to give and receive love, and it was wonderful to have all that feedback and celebration. We were in joyful shock. I told Mom that as usual she was an over-achiever, teacher's pet. She gets an A+ in cancer.

Her spirits are still up. She remains focused on gratitude and the future. She's just doing it quietly from bed with ginger chews by her side...It's not over yet. But we're close, very close. Amen and hallelujah!

THE HOLIDAYS

Advent 2015 dawned bleak on November 29 in Houston. Overcast. Drizzly. Bleh! Thanksgiving was behind us, its remnants still bulging in the fridge or piled in a corner to be put away. We were dealing with the aftermath now, my weary body struggling to cope with the effects of Prednisone ® and too many sleepless nights.

I could not fall asleep the night before. I was still up when it came time for Emi and Andy to leave at 4 a.m. The ride to the airport lulled me, and I finally fell asleep at about 5 a.m. for a couple of hours. Insomnia became my norm for Prednisone ®. When it wore off, it felt like falling off a cliff. It was hard to get up again. Welcome to week two of chemotherapy treatment. This is how it began every time. Every. Time.

Week two was the low week, the languish on the couch week. Lethargic. Unfocused. Mildly depressed. Whatever, I don't care week. Just let me lie here a while longer. My mood matched the bleak weather out my window.

I was right in time with the beginning of Advent, the 4-week period before Christmas. That morning, I realized I was in exile as much as the ancient Israelites who had been carried off to Babylon. They longed for a Savior. So did I. My way of life had been completely uprooted and turned around. I was living in a world of PICC lines and dressing changes, chemo jolts, and weird medications. Most days I was positive and optimistic. But this day I was still sugared up and exhausted. Yep. That's the beginning of Advent all right. Exile! Help! Someone save me! This is too hard!

As I wrote this I heard the strains of the familiar hymn that always begins this season: *O Come, O Come, Emmanuel, and ransom captive Israel, that mourns in lonely exile here, until the Son of God appears.*

What needed to happen in my life over here at my house before Christmas?

How would I celebrate in this homebound year when my spirit was often in the toilet and I was cloistered away?

I made a big push to get out to the farm for Thanksgiving. It was important to me. I needed to see all those people and to be on the land. I loved it, but that and the Prednisone® had taken their toll. I was wiped out, full of allergies and fighting some strange bug in my system. I monitored my temperature every hour. It was only up one degree, but if it climbed another, I would have to go to the hospital. Clearly, I could not do as much as I wanted to, even if I felt like it.

This time of year, I was usually all about the decorations, decisions about year-end charitable giving, parties, and gifts for my family. My birthday gets thrown into the mix. This year my birthday fell on the day after chemo—vomit day. Great! I was pondering. What would I have to do to be ready for Christmas? Anything? What was essential?

I knew shopping was not unless I bought things online. No Christmas concerts. No proud grandma moment at the graduation ceremony for granddaughter Emilie (bragging here—the first in our family to graduate from college *magna cum laude*!). No attendance at the ceremony awarding me my certificate in spiritual direction. No parties. As I wrote, my eyes started tearing up. Clearly, I would have to do something special, or I would weep through the next month.

How could I make it through the holidays, not simply to endure them, but to feel Christmas deeply within me? I thought first of the vital spiritual practices that had brought me enormous life so far: prayer, writing, kindergarten art, exercise. I needed a Christmas tree and a nativity set, maybe a few of my beloved nutcrackers.

Perhaps I needed to re-frame the holiday. Instead of focusing on what was missing that year, I should focus on something else. Oh, what to do! My mind would not focus.

The light came into my darkness in the form of a sweet minister friend, Noelie, who visited and brought gifts, music, cards, and advent supplies. How she blessed me, especially with a new insight into Scripture—from the gospel of Luke where Zechariah is struck mute for unbelief because he could not believe that his aged wife, Elizabeth, would bear a child, John the Baptist.

I saw that Scripture as punishment, God's being a little cruel. I mean, after all, if an angel showed up telling me that I would become pregnant at my age, I too would find that hard to believe. Anyone would. Why punish the guy for a natural, very human response? Not everything in the Bible makes sense to me.

Noelie shed some new light on this Scripture. What if being silent was a gift? What if his silence led him to a deep inner experience of the presence of God? Something profound and very spiritual must have been going on in all those mute months because the first words out of his mouth are a magnificent song of praise of God. It wasn't a curse at all. Instead the silence deepened his faith in a way that nothing else could.

I thought about my own life, those months of silence when I was homebound. Was I not living the Zechariah experience—a time of quiet when rich and deep things were going on in my spirit? Isn't that behind my descriptions of the cancer experience as a cocoon that will ultimately end in butterflies? Had I not felt the presence of God in fresh ways throughout those days lying on the couch in my living room?

Wow. Just wow. Suddenly I had a new and vibrant kinship with old Zechariah. God was preparing him to father a special child. This was indeed a time for both of us to reflect and grow in faith. God was preparing me for the days ahead, although it was too early to say what that would be. I hoped it was not a baby! I sensed this was a time for both of us, Zechariah and me, to reflect and grow in faith. I prayed that my first words after this cloistered life ended might also be a song of praise.

Indeed, the Scriptures that began this liturgical year pointed to a world gone nuts, yet told us to stand with our heads held high because we are being birthed into something brand new. God comes to us in these wild and terrifying times. Redemption draws near, and even as I wrote these words, I felt a little rustle of hope rising within me, like a tender shoot ready to push through the hard and frozen ground. Yes. Yes!

This would be an unusual advent to be sure. Fortunately, I knew the end of the story. I was sandwiched in between depression and glory, but glory would come. I knew it. I felt it.

I prayed it would be so for all of us on the journey to Bethlehem, and prayed we would all find the gifts of Advent: hope, peace, joy, and love.

TRAIN WRECK

For the last movie of 2015, I chose *Train Wreck* for our movie group. The choice raised a few eyebrows. Call it my Prednisone®, wild-eyed, crazy woman week. I thought about it long after the screen credits rolled and figured the film offered good fodder for conversation. It was, after all, nominated for a Golden Globe award.

I see movies for spiritual direction. I pay attention to what touches my heart, makes me angry, or stays with me long after the film has ended. I don't judge or evaluate movies critically. I think about the issues the film raises within me.

I like following Joseph Campbell's model of the hero's journey. It begins with a call to adventure that usually happens within the first 5 minutes of a movie. From there, the hero or heroine begins their journey by stepping onto the road of trials. Conflict happens. Grace appears. These two themes happen back and forth, and the heroine responds, either growing and transforming into a stronger character or falling into a despair of sorts. There is a climax, an all or nothing moment, followed by the denouement or a lesson that is learned and passed on.

In my earlier years, I lived with a terrible fear of the future. I thought things were only going to go downhill. My thoughts were negative. Prayer didn't seem to help much. Neither did the Bible. Scripture lay lifeless on the page. It never entered my heart, or if it did, it did not stay long.

I learned faith from the movies. Over and over, I saw the hero meet challenges. Always, grace appeared in some form on the road of trials. I came to believe that grace would also appear for me. I could trust that doors would open for me as it did for the main character in the film. I began to see parallels with Scripture. The Bible became relevant for me again.

Train Wreck tells the story of a young woman, named Amy. She is promiscuous, and her belief system tells her monogamy is wrong. She is in bed with someone different every night. She dresses in sexy, provocative ways. She drinks a lot. She works for a sleazy company, and she smokes pot. In one of the opening scenes, we see her early in the morning on the crowded Staten Island ferry in New York. She sports a revealing gold lamé short, SHORT mini skirt and stiletto heels and raises her hands in the air in triumph. She is living the dream. Her credo could be, "If it feels good, do it!" Her call to adventure begins when she meets a sports doctor, and we see her belief system challenged as they begin to fall in love. Amy must face her fears. I won't describe the end, but the movie raised all kinds of questions for me. What does the church have to say to people like her? Those are the kind of folks who hung out with Jesus after all. Can you imagine her sitting on a church pew? Hardly.

Because it was New Year's Eve, I was looking at Amy's belief system that had stopped working for her. That begged the question for me: What outdated belief system did I need to let go of to enter a new year? January and the end of chemotherapy offered a great opportunity.

For sure I was letting go of the notion that I would never get cancer. I always thought I was immune—that I would die suddenly from a heart attack. I may still drop dead from a heart attack, but I may not. I was wrong about that. What else could I be wrong about?

I have spent a lot of time beating myself up over the years for not being perfect, for lollygagging, and for not accomplishing more. I also put others ahead of myself by not taking time to exercise and not caring for myself well. Those things formed a powerful gateway for lymphoma, I think, and I needed to let them go.

One of the larger misbeliefs I needed to discard in the new year was the ancient belief that exercise would kill me. I could let go of that belief easier if I were charmed away from it like Amy in *Train Wreck*. No, I don't mean a handsome, rich sports doctor. I mean the kind of exercise I could really look forward to, something I could fall in love with, something I felt eager to do. That was my hope for a New Year's resolution—to fall in love with ways of moving my body that would be life-giving. Then I could let go of a belief system no longer serving me.

I was curious whether anyone in my movie group would take the bait that night and be willing to talk about letting go in the new year. Sometimes when I ask them personal questions, they change the subject and refuse to answer the question I asked. That's OK. I got what I needed out of *Train Wreck*. Other people may have heard the voice of the Spirit saying something completely different to them. That was not uncommon. I always looked forward to the discussion, and I was usually enriched by it as I saw how the Spirit hovers over peoples' lives.

I missed going to movies. I missed having people over to talk about them. I hoped that in February I would feel well enough to sit in theaters and watch the films being nominated for the Academy Awards. A brand-new world would open for me after my last chemotherapy treatment on the following Monday, January 4, in a brand-new year. I hoped to be careful about what I needed to let go and what I needed to add.

DOES GRATITUDE WORK?

I loathed chemotherapy and its aftermath, and those feelings were getting stronger as the final treatment approached during the month of December 2015. I was in remission, but Dr. Turturro insisted it was necessary to complete the six-treatment cycle. I hated it. I abhorred it, especially during the first 5 days of it when I took Prednisone® and experienced all its nasty side effects—rampant insomnia, weight gain, moon face, ugh!

One of the tricks they taught me at MD Anderson was not letting my thoughts head off in the wrong direction. Stop them in their tracks before they mow you down. Learn to live with gratitude. That's hard to do with 3 hours sleep.

December 30, 2015, was one of those days where all the images in my head were like volcanoes erupting—lots of anger going on! I hated chemotherapy! Dread and despair descended.

What if my life would be like this forever? Without energy. Listless on the couch. I told myself:

I am weary of it!

I am weary of things piling up and neglected tasks.

I am weary, period!

Help me, God! I feel so useless!

Perhaps gratitude would help me turn the corner. It often did. I took pen in hand and began to write 10 things for which I was grateful that morning. Forcing myself, I laid them out.

1. I was grateful to be older and retired. I could not imagine feeling like this and having children underfoot or a job somewhere.

2. I was grateful to live in Houston, where the temperatures are balmy in winter, not freezing.

3. I was grateful for good insurance. Say what you will about socialized medicine, but Medicare is a blessing. So is the pension plan of the Presbyterian Church USA.

4. I was grateful for a loving family and their patience with my limitations.

5. I was grateful we had spruced up the downstairs of our home several years ago. It looked pretty to me and filled me with peace.

6. I was grateful for Sydney, an old dog whose energy level matched my own. A puppy would have driven me nuts. Sydney was very sweet and did not have many annoying habits.

7. I was grateful for Amazon. Stuck in my house, I could still shop online and purchase everything from vitamins to underwear.

8. I was grateful to have a sense of humor. Among my new year's resolutions was laughter. I needed to lighten up!

9. Although I was not wild about insomnia, I felt grateful to see a sunrise every morning. I loved greeting the day with

my journal and a cup of coffee. I had a fresh, blank slate every morning ripe with possibility.

10. I was grateful not to be alone in traveling the journey of cancer. Being vulnerable online felt awkward sometimes, but the payoff was remarkable, thanks to friends, family, Facebook, and Caring Bridge. I felt buoyed and lifted by love, prayers, and support.

Writing all of this down helped me turn the corner. No longer surly, I had felt the shift within my spirit from anger to peace, even joy. This simple exercise taught me a lesson: Gratitude really does work!

THE MESSAGE IN THE MOUNTAINS

My hand still hurt where they stuck the needle in February 2017. It was a horrible, painful stick, the worst of all the gazillion times I had been stuck. It made me wince and scream out loud, but I expected everything to be fine with the CT scan. No problem. I was on this fancy drug that was designed to keep me in remission for 2 years. Time enough to cross off most of the items on my bucket list and have a grand celebration at the end of it. Plenty of time. Or that's what I thought.

"There is no cause for alarm," Dr. Turturro said. "A few of the lymph nodes are growing—one in your clavicle area and another larger one in your stomach. We'll do another CAT scan in 2 months. If those places are growing, we will do a biopsy. Then there are several options. There are a number of clinical trials where you qualify." Fine just fine.

I knew I had a squirrely cancer the day I was diagnosed with follicular lymphoma. It comes and goes. All the time. It never really goes away and can pop out any time. There is no cure, just remission, meaning it has settled down, maybe hiding where it cannot be seen. But I was taking the miracle drug, Rituxan®. I had read that relapse from follicular lymphoma generally occurs at 7 months, but not with Rituxan®. One would have 2 years free and clear on Rituxan®. Not for me apparently. That was the hard part, the part that

I was angry! I had tried so hard to live healthy and take precautions. It all seemed for naught. I blamed myself. What would I do about the book I was writing on how I had kicked cancer's butt? I had not kicked cancer's butt very well if it had returned in 13 months. Sure, I sailed through chemotherapy with minimal side effects—no ugly fingernails, no peripheral neuropathy (except for a quarter-sized patch on my foot), no weight loss (unfortunately). I guessed it had morphed into a book about recovery and relapse. Shit! This really sucked.

The crazy thing was that I had been feeling great, Maybe it was the spring. Maybe it was a wonderful massage therapist. Maybe it was getting better sleep, or the exercise I had begun. Maybe all of it was working together.

What in the world would I do? It felt exhausting to think about. I was beyond disappointed. In prayer, I surrendered to God—again. "Lead me in your light," I prayed. "I am your child. Please help." Eloquent words eluded me, and in my mind, I was thinking:

> *I still have those three states to visit;*
>
> *the book to write, now dealing with relapse;*
>
> *the aurora borealis to see.*
>
> *And now I must deal with this! Give me strength, Lord. I am not ready to do this again. I humbly ask for your healing.*

I knew I was bargaining. *Let these things happen before I have to check out.* This new suspicion had not been confirmed medically. Dr. Turturro said, "Let's wait another month and see what happens. See if they continue to grow. We'll do another CT scan then and see. Maybe it's nothing."

My mind raced. *But what if it's something? What if the lymphoma has returned?*

The next day they posted my medical exams online. I accessed the MD Anderson portal and typed in my password. Sipping my decaf coffee, I quickly searched the results of my CAT scan. "Several cells appear rounded and clustered consistent with lymphoma," it read. "It appears like lymphoma," spelled out brutally clear in black and white. Suddenly there was no wiggle room. I accepted it as fact. The cancer was back. The eventual biopsies would just confirm which kind of lymphoma it was. Follicular lymphoma often morphs into something else. Like I say, it's a squirrely cancer.

In my mind's eye, I saw a frightened child. She was Little Patty, my inner child. I asked her, "How are you feeling?" "Terrified," she told me while shaking.

So that's it. My clearing of clutter, the shopping, the overeating were all coming from a place of fear, a place I tried to avoid. This was not the first time fear surfaced in my life. This was a pattern happening all the time until I was finally ready to sit with it and allow the fear to tell its story.

I asked what Little Patty needed from me. "Hold me," she said. "Help me feel better." We sat there together in the silence, Little Patty and me, in my mind's eye. I felt peace descend. It was going to be all right, for now, but I knew this fear was big and would return. I would have to repeat the process many times.

I remembered a recent conversation I had with an elderly woman at my church. I had preached that morning, and after changing out of my robe, I poured myself a cup of coffee and sat down on a couch in the gathering area next to this woman. She told me how much she had loved my sermon on laughter. "I have a friend who needs to hear this," she told me. "She will love it. You haven't preached in a while, and it was so good to have you back today."

"I have been trying to recover from cancer," I told her. "Oh," she said dryly and waved her hand as if to dismiss my comment. "I get that all the time. It's no big deal. I have had it three times already."

What an attitude I thought to myself! On this day when I was struggling with relapse, I thought about her and that attitude. No big deal. I liked that. No step for a stepper. Thinking about her, now well into her upper 80s, made me smile. So positive. So full of life. So full of joy. I loved it. I made the decision. *I want to be like her when I grow up.* "I get that all the time. No big deal."

Several days later my ministry colleague friends came over for our monthly lunch and art making. I passed out magazines of *Southwest Art* and told them to leaf through until a picture "shimmered" for them. I told them when they found it, to spend a minute looking at which part of it drew their attention and to look at it very carefully. After that, they were to expand their awareness to the rest of the picture by looking at the details, colors, and shapes. They should notice what they saw and what they felt emotionally. This process would take about 5 minutes after they found their picture; then they were to give it a title and begin to write what they saw and felt.

My picture was of the orange mountains of New Mexico. There were a few black shadows scattered on the sides of the mountain. This is what I wrote:

> *It leaps out at me, sucking up the entire space*
>
> *my beloved mountains of the west*
>
> *standing there strong and tall.*
>
> *It speaks to me of strength*
>
> *"Be strong and courageous..." is the Scripture that comes to mind*
>
> *except that the strength is within me*
>
> *standing tall*
>
> *able to withstand the ravages of time and disease.*
>
> *Only then do I notice there are clouds behind the cliffs*
>
> *powerful clouds.*
>
> *The Transfiguration appears in my awareness*
>
> *when the clouds overshadowed Jesus, Moses, and Elijah.*
>
> *It speaks to my heart this day of God's powerful presence hovering above me.*
>
> *And then there is this black—the sky and the shadows.*
>
> *Cancer jumps into my mind—spots of cancer!*

Will the darkness of the sky and shadows overtake the mountains?

I think not.

Not this time.

One of my minister friends pointed out that the two massive clouds appeared to be women's breasts. I wasn't so sure until I remembered one of the Hebrew words for God, *El Shaddai*, the God of the mountains. It can also mean the God of the breasts, the lovely feminine presence of God that makes everything shine and sparkle. It was one of my very favorite images for God. A simple picture. Mountains. Breasts. The healing presence of God. A reason why art is so powerful.

I quit overeating, quit shopping, quit running around in angst. My spirit was at peace until the next jolt of news would appear.

THINGS I NEVER SAID TO MY DOCTOR, FRANCESCO TURTURRO

1. Oh, what a wonderful, wonderful Italian accent!
2. I want to hear all about your journey to America—what made you come?
3. Do you have a wife?
4. A family?
5. Why don't you ever smile?
6. Do you ever show any emotion? You have such a flat affect.
7. Why did you choose to study lymphoma?
8. What interests you?
9. What do you do in your spare time?
10. Why are you so serious?
11. You are always in such a hurry to leave. Why is that?

12. Is there joy in your life?

13. I am following you now on Twitter. It seems you are a great liberal. Can we talk about that?

14. I notice that you are bald now in this visit. Is that a fashion statement?

15. Why can you not answer any of my questions? You think every single body part requires a visit to a different kind of doctor. I thought you were supposed to help with side effects.

16. Why can't you take my questions seriously? You are always in a big hurry to get out of here.

17. What is that pink stuff all over your head and arms? Do you have shingles?

18. Are you losing weight?

19. Why can't you ever sit down to talk to me? You look like you are ready to bolt every time you come into this room. You just stand there beside the door or the cabinet. Would it really kill you to sit down?

20. You are really losing a lot of weight. I wish I could do that.

21. Your new Twitter profile picture sucks. The pink shirt does not match the plaid blue shorts. You look dorky. Your white coat makes you look much more handsome.

22. I don't understand much of what you write on Twitter or the studies you refer to. You are obviously not writing for lay people. I sense a little arrogance here. Do you think you are smarter than most people? After all, you are a full professor at a prestigious medical school.

23. I looked you up online where I found your salary listed as $315,000 annually.

24. You have some fairly negative reviews. One guy said you would not answer his questions when he brought up supplements. You just bolted out the door without answering or saying goodbye. Outta there! Done! So I am not alone in thinking you lack a bedside manner.

25. Here's a good thing about you. You let me do whatever I want. I want to participate in Livestrong. You sign off on it. I want massage. You refer me to integrative medicine. I want acupuncture. Fine with you. Nutrition consult? Check. Psychological counseling? Check. Fatigue clinic. You write the order (or your assistant did).

26. You have never denied me anything I ever wanted to do and honor all my requests.

27. You are even slimmer this visit than you were the last one. You are starting to look like a skeleton.

28. I have decided that you are brilliant and well organized, and I would rather have brilliance when it comes to cancer treatment than pastoral care. A lot of cancer doctors are really, really smart when it comes to science but not so great at bedside manner. You are one of those, and that's nally ok with me. I have lots of places where I can get someone to listen to me.

29. You sat down to talk to me today. I felt honored. You told me the results of my CT scan are not great—nothing to worry about yet. If the cancer has returned there are clinical trials for which I can qualify. I said, "I am counting on you to take care of me." You smiled and looked away. I knew right then that the bald head, the shingles, the profound weight loss means you have cancer and apparently a rather advanced case of it. We have never spoken of your health or physical appearance, and we do not speak of it now.

30. I got a letter from MD Anderson today. It says that you are no longer seeing patients at MD Anderson. They wish you well in your future endeavors. Why can you not talk about this? I feel uneasy.

31. I called MD Anderson, a little panicky about my care. They tell me I have been assigned to a Dr. Fayad. Do I go through with my CT scan? I feel strangely disjointed and nervous. I mean, you are no genius at pastoral care, but I always trusted you to give me the right treatment.

32. I sit in the lobby of the lymphoma clinic waiting to meet Dr. Fayad. I overhear nurses talking to one another. Their tone is hushed. They say you died this morning.

33. I meet Dr. Fayad, whom I like very much. He tells me that you had diagnosed me correctly and prescribed the proper treatment for a cancer as advanced as mine. "Do you know who I would see if I had lymphoma?" he asks me. "no, who?" I respond. "Me!" he says emphatically. "I am the best!" "Do you know where I would go if I were not available?" "Where?" I ask him. "Dr. Turturrro!" he says. He obviously thinks a lot about you.

34. "How did Dr. Turturro die?" I question. "Pancreatic cancer," he tells me. "He was a good man. He worked until the end."

35. I am reeling with this news—no closure, no farewell to any of your patients, nurses, or office workers apparently. Why? You were always private, too private in my book.

36. You come to me. I sense your presence in my spirit, but I am pissed off. You apologize to me for blowing me off. You promise to guide me through the new process of treatment. I don't want to hear it. I am furious with you for dying and not saying a word about it. You linger.

37. I read your obituary in the newspaper. You are survived by your high school sweetheart whom you married back in Italy. You had two children and a grandson. Friends and family are invited to visitation and rosary and a mass the following day. I decide we are neither friends nor family, so I don't go. Your presence still lingers. You promise to look after me. I am still angry. I won't talk to you.

38. It's been several months now. Your presence is gone. I am not angry anymore. I'm sorry I did not go to your service. Thank you for your care of me.

39. I miss you.

THE VIOLIN PLAYER

The painting called to me one day from the back pages of *Southwest Art* magazine, my favorite when it comes to art journaling. Sitting on a makeshift stool, the elderly gray-haired man was playing a mandolin or violin type of thing. Maybe homemade. Hunched over as though it were a cello, he played with his eyes closed, lost in the wonder of his music. I could almost hear the sound of strings. It was a remarkable 11 x 14 oil pastel that coincidentally had been painted by Forrest's cousin, Neva Rossi.

For that day's art project, I had chosen a few 5 x 7 blank cards, and written a question on the back of each one of them. I turned them over and shuffled them, so I did not know what was written on the back, then painted the front side with watercolors. The watercolors were the background, and each one was different. I cut out different designs for each one of them too, making primitive collages. On one of them, I pasted a tree on the card, then glued the cutout picture of the violin player underneath it. I was startled when I finished gluing and turned it over. My primitive design was the surprising answer to the question, "What is my purpose in life?"

Right then I knew that my purpose in life is to be creative again. I had long felt that I lost all creativity through the process of becoming a minister.

To become ordained in my tradition means rigorous study and testing. Presbyterians live in their heads. We're smart. We have a higher percentage of college graduates per capita than most denominations. Our brainy strength is also a great weakness. We don't focus on the heart and soul. Sometimes we seem out of balance, or I can anyway. So many words!

I knew that I had to buy that original art pastel of the violin player. Forrest and I visited Neva and picked it up on our way to a family reunion. Neva told me the story of the aged man. She was visiting Venice, Italy, and encountered him on the sunlit piazza, all by himself, playing his makeshift instrument. The church bells on the square began to ring, and as they did, he closed his eyes and continued to play. He was lost in the music of his strings. So profoundly moved watching him, she pulled out her camera, snapped his picture, and came home where she recreated him on canvas.

That gentle man had spent the morning sitting there doing his creative thing, unworried about what anyone thought, not judging his effort, not paying attention to anyone else, only playing that instrument as though his life depended upon it. Maybe it did. Now, what does all of this have to do with cancer? Let me explain.

Lucia Capacchione maintains that the body is a great storyteller and contains unbelievable wisdom if we will listen. She healed herself of a disease that threatened to kill her years ago by drawing images on paper and dialoguing with them. After my relapse, I pulled out my journal and markers and drew the part of my body where the cancer was the worst. I then asked with the nondominant hand: "Who are you?"

The nondominant hand wrote: *I am your pelvic area filling with cancer.*

"How are you feeling?" I returned to my dominant hand.

The answer startled me: *I am lonely. I am empty inside, so I invited the cancer to keep me company. I miss growing babies and being creative.*

"What do you want me to do for you?" *Do something creative every day. You have let that part of you fall by the wayside. Pick it up again! Create!*

Create! Create! Let that become your priority. Write. Collage. Learn to draw. Make art cards. Go through Lucia's books again. You spend too much time on the computer.

"What are you here to teach me?" *To be your creative self.*

I hung the painting of the violin player on the red wall in my living room. He sits directly in my line of sight across from the comfortable brown couch where I spend so much time. That elderly musician speaks to me every day now by his very presence. "Do something creative," he whispers. "It will bring you life." Somehow my healing is tied up with his message.

GO TO HELL

If I make my bed in Sheol (hell), you are there. (Psalm 139:8)

I went to hell on the Fourth of July 2017. It's just as bad as you would imagine.

I never wondered much about hell—figured it was a place for terrorists and evil people, not someone like me who had been vaccinated against it. You know the vaccine—accept Christ as your Savior, and voila! All terror is eliminated. No more worries about evil and devils as we glide through life in bliss. I don't think that's true anymore.

I've always said heaven begins on earth—those moments of ecstasy that give us a glimpse into God's beauty and grace. But hell! I just tried to stay away from the habits that would bring me there, the continual turning away from God.

I started chemotherapy again the first week of July 2017. It seemed easier. I had great energy for a few days afterward. I could hardly believe my good fortune. "Piece of cake," I thought. By Friday the experience turned sour. Nausea engulfed me. I ached everywhere. My energy level plummeted. We missed the big Fourth of July parade in Shiner. I could barely sit up. When I realized I was running a fever, Forrest and I headed to the emergency room at MD Anderson.

They admitted me, and by then I had uncontrollable vomiting. It took 5 hours to get it under control, even with several intravenous medications. Was I surrounded by God's love and grace? Yes. Did I feel it? No. Hell no. It was the worst night of my life.

The kind nurse asked me, "Have you ever had suicidal thoughts?"

"Yes," I told her. "Right now."

She looked very concerned. "Do you think you would intentionally do something to hurt yourself?"

"No," I told her. "I don't have the courage. But I would be open to being shot."

More vomiting. It was the pits. I was in hell.

The Christian vaccine wasn't helping much. Yes, I was surrounded by loving, caring people, but nothing was working. It was the longest night of my life. So yeah, I think we have hell on earth. Lots of people are there right now. I learned a few things that night, now that I am on the other side of it.

- *I'm no hero.*

- *Platitudes did not help.*

- *Scripture did not help.*

- *Advice, except from the medical team, did not help.*

- *The gentle prayer offered by the Vietnamese chaplain did. Greatly.*

- *Quiet, responsible people doing their jobs did.*

- *Forrest's quiet presence beside me did.*

- *Lots of people are in hell right now.*

It turns out I had the flu, not a chemotherapy reaction and not an infection. The biggest takeaway from my 3 days at MD Anderson is that I needed to start taking this disease and its treatment seriously. I blew cancer off when I relapsed, treated it like a nuisance. I was not afraid of it. I did not think lymphoma would kill me, not then anyway, but I realized I needed to make some alterations to my lifestyle. It was probably a bad idea to go grocery shopping after chemotherapy. I never washed my hands afterward. I needed to be more mindful.

The first time I went through chemo I lived in a bubble. I did not want to do that again. It made me crazy to think about. I needed to decide what my new normal would look like. For sure, I did not want to land in hell again.

As a child, I thought hell was a scary place of fire. When I grew older, I thought hell would be living without the presence of God. I don't think either of those things anymore. God is always around. God never leaves us. Sometimes though, like that horrible July night in the hospital, we don't see or experience God's presence. That does not mean that God is not there. It's like the starry nights out at my farm in Shiner. Some nights they are beautiful and glittering and fill us with awe and wonder. Other nights are cloudy, and we cannot see them. That doesn't mean they are not there. It's just that we cannot see.

How did hell change me? I have a deeper compassion now for all those who are in it. I am grateful to be alive, to have such a fine, fine family, and to be the recipient of the world's best medical care. I am grateful for the love of God who will never let us go. Scripture tells us, "Weeping endures for the night, but joy comes in the morning." I am especially grateful that the long night ended as I embrace the joy of a new day.

THE LITTLE THINGS

"You are so elegant," she told me. "Your hair, the color of your shirt, your earrings, your shoes, even your toenails. You are very elegant." The sweet nurse was prepping me with jelly for a sonogram of the veins in my arms. Little did she know how non-elegant I felt, but how susceptible I am to flattery. It felt good to have a compliment.

The chemotherapy ward had sent me to her after two unsuccessful attempts to find a vein for the IV. That nurse had come from Dallas, sent to MD Anderson on a busload of nurses to help out in the aftermath of Harvey. She failed twice in her efforts to find a vein, then sent me to the sonogram room. In that suite, they do a sonogram of your arm to find a vein, then stick the needle into the vein that shows on the screen. "Look! It's smiling at you," she said. Unfortunately, both tries failed, and she went to find Pilar. Pilar is apparently a living legend around those parts of MD Anderson. Pilar came in, found a vein, stuck in a big needle, and then taped it to my arm. I was good to go after this, the fifth of my sticks.

By now it was 6:30 p.m. and time to begin my 6-hour chemo. I had been there since 2:30. The process of dripping the pricey liquids into my veins was uneventful other than the transfer to the main building when the clinic I was in closed for the night. They parked me in a wheelchair, planted the IV tree between my legs, and told me to hold on. I did. They walked me over the sky bridge and into the warm smile of another wonderful nurse working the late shift.

That long night, I began to dream of travel. Years ago, I had forsaken trips overseas because of the lengthy airline flights. Now I thought, "If I can lie in bed practically immobile for hours on end, I can endure a long airplane ride."

Sometimes I get weary of all the snafus at MD Anderson. I get so tired of waiting. There are days I say to myself, "This is the number one cancer hospital in the world?"

What made the MD Anderson experience worthwhile to me were the nurses, especially the Filipino nurses. One of them told me that night, "Caring is in our nature. It's who we are." The young Filipino nurse in the sonogram room had made my day by giving me a compliment. I did not even mind the extra sticks trying to get a good vein after that.

I have learned that it's the little things in life that make the difference:

A smile

A compliment

A card or a text

They allow the light to come in when people are lonely or afraid. Simple things don't require a lot of effort and can make someone feel so much better. Maybe I can do more of that.

They are teaching me at MD Anderson and not just about the drugs that drip into my body. They are showing me a way of healing that manifests all the fruits of the Spirit of God by how they treat people. I am grateful.

F. Scott Fitzgerald once wrote, "It was only a sunny smile, and little it cost in the giving, but like morning light it scattered the night and made the day worth living."

I resolved to keep smiling.

HOW CANCER HAS CHANGED ME

After the fourth chemotherapy treatment in October 2017, I was sick of it. My legs stiffened. Nausea stalked me. Fatigue crippled me. I was back on the couch. "This can only get worse," I thought.

"It's dormant," the nurse had told me after the third treatment. "There is no evidence of disease now, but it will come back. This cancer is incurable." In my mind, I started to question my treatment plan. *Why should I continue this chemo if I am already in remission? Why make myself feel even worse?*

At my next appointment, I asked the nurse why I needed to continue.

"It's the protocol," he said. "O-Bendamustine® is administered six times."

"But what if I want to stop after four? Can I do that?"

"The protocol is six treatments," he told me.

"What happens if you stop early?" I asked.

"There are no studies for that," he told me. "They all involve six treatments; you need to finish."

"The chemotherapy is making me feel bad," I told him. "I am already in remission, and I want to stop."

"I think that's a bad idea," he said. "You need to finish."

"Why not start a new study?" I asked him.

"You will have to speak with the doctor," he said.

My husband was in the room with me. He was quiet, but he too believed strongly I needed to finish the next two chemotherapies.

Nurse Justin remained seated at the small desk when Dr. Fayad came in with a couple of medical students. The doctor introduced me to them.

"I don't want any more chemo," I told him. "I want to stop. It's making me feel bad, like R-CHOP did in the first round. I am already in remission. I have booked a cruise to the Mediterranean for January, and I will not be able to go if I continue treatment."

He looked at me hard and paused a minute. "OK," he said. "I don't want to make you sick. When is your trip?"

"January," I told him.

"Do you have insurance for the trip?"

"Yes."

"I want you to have a scan before you go."

"OK," I said. We shook hands, and he was out the door.

He had no idea that a monumental shift had occurred within me. I grew up with the belief that people in authority must always be obeyed. My voice was silenced again and again as a child until I finally learned to play by the rules. Standing up for myself was a new thing, but that day I made the shift. I am not afraid to stand up for myself anymore.

Lots of changes have happened in my life since then. Cancer has a way of revealing one's priorities. Knowing for certain that my time on earth is limited, perhaps as few as 5 years, makes life even more precious. I don't have many regrets. I wish I had played more with my children when they were young and spent more quality time with the family. I am grateful to have time for them now. I wish I had taken some art classes instead of drill team in high school. I discarded a lot of myself just trying to be popular, and it never worked.

I am still doing art and teaching the methods to others. I am no longer ashamed of nor embarrassed by it. I think most people are afraid of doing art. They stopped emphasizing it in the first grade in my school, and I think that's the case for many of us. We feel awkward about drawing stick figures and showing them to anyone else.

The art that Lucia taught me has nothing to do with beauty. It's all about getting what's going on within us outside of us and onto the page. Allowing a primitive, crudely drawn picture to tell its story was a huge path to my healing–both times. I will never stop doing it. It was the most supportive thing I did and continue to do throughout the cancer experience. It became my constant companion because it was so simple. It reminded me that God loved me, assured me that I would be OK, and gave me profound insights that healed my psyche.

My world is a little smaller since chemotherapy. A lot of things put me in over-whelm. I lack the patience to put up with many matters that I once did: people who drain me; world situations I cannot solve; hard books; too much talking, especially when the conversation is superficial and uninteresting; large gath-erings of people; negativity in general, unless it's funny; and financial affairs. I have become an introvert.

Chemo accelerated the aging process. I now have age spots, wrinkles, and thinning hair. I lost all my hair after the first chemotherapy, but it came back gray, thick, and curly. I did not know what color my hair was naturally. I had not seen it in years. The Bendamustine® the second time around was supposed to thin the hair, and they promised me the locks would all come back as they were. Wrong! I am still shedding like a dog. Thank goodness my hair is curly!

For the most part, people treat me the same as they always did, although I lost a few friends. They just disappeared. Some people are disappointed that I don't spring into action like I did in the old days whenever they had a problem. Others have been in pretty dire straits, and I have done nothing to help meet their needs. I have ignored a lot of things, but I have less energy than I used to. I must put my health needs first. There are days that I feel lifeless and guilty that I am not doing more in the world to make a difference. On those days, an inner voice whispers to me, *You can write. You can do that and make a difference, even if it is small.*

I was never angry with God during the whole experience. I figured God was the constant that would help me get through it. My prayer life is not as flowery as it used to be. It's become as primitive as my art, but I have some music and devotional books that help. Centering prayer and meditation have become my norm. Mostly I feel a lot of gratitude, and I am learning to live one day at a time. What I look forward to is traveling as I check off my bucket list of places I need to see before I quite literally kick the bucket. I am weary of writing about cancer and other hard things. I am looking forward to more travel and writing about that. Adventure has always made my spirit come alive!

A bright green beanie baby frog during a writing retreat in Boulder, Colorado, triggered a memory of a day in December 2015 when I lay on the couch, full of chemo and waiting for the "red zinger" drug to exit my body. As I lay there, I felt completely in my own space, unaware of anything going on beside me. I sensed a subtle loosening of all that surrounded me. It was as though attachments to people, my home and its contents all gently floated away. I was in my own little world, unable to move much, but not wanting to move at all. I did not care if I ever moved again. I was a part of this world but not really. It was surreal.

The thought entered my mind, *Oh, this is what it feels like to die from cancer.* This isn't so bad. I can do this. I knew then that I was unafraid to die and unafraid to let go when the time came. In the same moment, I knew this was not the hour of my death. I knew I would survive this chemo and maybe several others before my time came to pass. In those remarkable minutes of relaxing my attachments, I experienced a glimpse of release that was gentle, peaceful and loving. I felt gently warmed within my body. I was unafraid and felt confident that I could meet the challenge of death with grace.

I held that beanie baby frog on a sunny summer afternoon in Boulder and remembered my childhood when I used to be terrified of frogs. I would shriek and run for cover if one ever crossed my path. Now I am unafraid of frogs. I still don't want to pick them up and play with them, but I can walk around them without screaming. It's more like stepping to the side naturally and wordlessly when something blocks one's path. I realized looking at that stuffed green frog, that just as I no longer feared him or his kind, I no longer fear death. When the time comes, I will be ready. It will come gently, and I will glide into it.

WHERE I AM NOW

In January 2018 I had another CT scan. It was fine. There was still no evidence of disease. Dr. Fayad said, "Go out and live your life. Have a good time. Come back in 6 months." "Yay!" I thought, "6 months with no chemo! Freedom!" The next week I got on a boat and went to the Mediterranean.

I had booked the tour with one of my favorite clergywomen. After Rome, Pompeii, and Palermo we docked in Mallorca on January 23, 2018. Margaret said, "Let's go somewhere!" We piled into an air-conditioned bus and headed for the Dragon Caves, not sure exactly what we would find. When we entered the musty, humid cave with a couple of hundred other people it looked like we were standing inside a big hunk of Swiss cheese, only it wasn't yellow. It was more like a beige, brown color. "Be careful on those stone steps," Margaret warned me. "They're hard to see." It was humid and probably about 80 degrees. Carefully, we weaved our way downward on the dimly lit path. The only light came from spotlights shining in the "holes" of the cheese and illuminating the stalactites and stalagmites. "Here, let me take your picture," she said near one of the holes with a lot of the needle-like formations. Some of them were spectacular. None of the pictures turned out well because of the darkness. We could not tarry as there were multitudes of people crawling their way in behind us.

We made it down the 144 steps, then entered an enormous barely lit cavern at the bottom. It was wet and slippery. I felt triumphant that I was doing OK health wise, scarcely missing a beat. They ushered us onto long wooden benches. Before us was a lighted and beautiful turquoise colored lake, one of the largest underground lakes in the world. It was perfectly still. The backdrop was a rugged rock formation full of icicle-looking stalactites. The lake meandered through another cavern off to the right where we could not see.

After about a 10-minute wait, the loudspeaker came on in several languages. In English, we heard, "Please do not take any pictures. Please be silent. Please, no flashbulbs of any kind." Then they turned out the lights in that huge, high ceilinged cavern, and we sat in silence. I shivered with anticipation.

From a distance, I heard the faint and gentle sounds of violins playing Pachelbel's canon. Someone whispered, "Do you hear it? I can't see anything." Slowly, ever so slowly, three lighted rowboats quietly came into view, and four musicians weaved their magic, filling the air with gorgeous, enchanting music. The hair on my arms stood on end. Spellbound, mesmerized watching them, I almost held my breath. The musicians, playing violins and cello, were in one boat. Another boat sailed in front of them and one behind them. They glided to the end of the lake that seemed to be double the length of a football field, then gently returned, playing classical music all the while in that darkened place. The impact was stunning! It was sublime. My spirit soared beyond the very top of the cavern into the realm of heaven it seemed. Soon the boats sailed out of sight. The subdued lights came on. It was over, but not for me. Beauty had planted itself in my heart.

Margaret and I climbed up the shadowy stairs in silence. We walked out into a bright, beautiful day, transformed.

A person next to me said, "Wow, that was something!" "Yeah," I said. "It was."

Margaret and I never learned why they are called the dragon caves. Many people believe dragons symbolize wisdom, longevity, and renewal. I have that to look forward to as I regain my strength. Just as I had endured long months of chemotherapy and been declared in remission, for now, the cave was a metaphor for walking out of darkness and into the light. I turned a corner that beckoned me into a new life without cancer.

As I found beauty and grace in the dimness of that cave, I knew that grace would accompany me wherever I went, even in the night. Just as the chemo had healed my body, again, the Dragon Caves of Mallorca healed my soul.

To God be the glory, now and forever.

FEELING
THE
SHIFT

Gallery

I WILL SING

I will sing and make melody to the Lord. (Psalm 27:6)

Who are you?
I am Patty, all grown up and singing her heart out.

What is your message to me?
I am teaching you how to play. You missed that part for a lot of your childhood. I am helping you find that part of yourself that has been hidden for a long, long time.

What do you need from me?
Let me be 5 years old again. I will bring you a new life. Let it out. Don't be afraid.

LAND OF THE LIVING

*I believe that I shall see the goodness of the Lord
in the land of the living.* (Psalm 27:13)

When I thought about "the land of the living," I pictured a world
of diversity, creativity, divinity, peace, groundedness, passion, and
beauty. I added a butterfly, a symbol of the resurrection in the
middle to illustrate the belief that it is coming. When I finished, I
held it to the Lord with a prayer that it would happen.

IN THE SPOTLIGHT

Oh Lord, you have searched me and known me. (Psalm 139:1)

When I meditated on this verse, the first image was of a spotlight shining on me—Gods healing light. But it had no warmth. As I pondered the image, suddenly it changed to Jesus, washing Peter's feet. Peter could only sit and receive as Jesus ministered to him. It was difficult for him to receive without giving in return. This has always been difficult for me too.

Receiving so much love from my family and friends during treatment, although difficult in the beginning, has been the lasting image from the cancer experience. It has indeed been God's healing light pouring into my body.

A WARM BEACH

You know when I sit down and when I rise up.
You discern my thoughts from far away. You search out my path
and my lying down and are acquainted with all my ways.
(Psalm 139:2-3)

It was a chilly day in October when I fashioned this,
imagining myself on a warm beach with the sunlight
streaming onto my body. I held it to God in prayer,
asking for the healing warmth of the Spirit to enfold me.

BLAH
BLAH
BLAH

BLAH, BLAH, BLAH

Even before a word is on my tongue, O Lord,
you know it completely. (Psalm 139:4)

It was one of those mornings when I was whiny and negative.
Every word I formed was a complaint. I fashioned this head
wearing my pink knit cap, sparkling 4-leaf clover earrings, and a
giant tongue. I could hear a voice within me saying, in effect, "I've
heard it all, Pat. I am here." I made a deliberate switch to gratitude.

WHEN I CONSIDER
YOUR HEAVENS

Such knowledge is too wonderful for me;
it is so high that I cannot attain it. (Psalm 139:6)

In my mind, I saw a starry night and the beauty of God's creation.
It reminded me of the greatness and sovereignty of God who
has promised good to us. Deliberately focusing on something
greater than myself placed me in a higher realm emotionally.
I began to praise God.

THE INNER LIGHT

Where can I go from your Spirit?
Or where can I flee from your presence? (Psalm 139:7)

The Spirit of God resides within each of us.
Wherever we are, God is in this beautiful, technicolor world.

AT THE EDGE OF THE SEA

*If I take the wings of the morning and settle at the farthest
limits of the sea, even there your hand shall lead me,
and your right hand shall hold me fast.* (Psalm 139:7)

My default position spiritually often assumes everything depends
on me. The picture of the house at the very edge of the sea, almost
out of sight, reminds me that I cannot run away from God; I cannot
sail away from God; I cannot write God out of my life; God does not
abandon his children. God is wherever I am and holds me close,
even if I fail to perceive it.

CONFIDENCE

I praise you, for I am fearfully and wonderfully made.
(Psalm 139:14)

This drawing, made in early November 2016, resembles the
initial Little Patty drawing made earlier in my treatment.
Whereas Little Patty was tentative and fearful of being pummeled,
this one shows some progress. She's a little more confident.
I was learning to love my inner child.

ACKNOWLEDGMENTS

I feel profound gratitude for all of those who helped me in the process of getting this book published.

CaringBridge provided a powerful tool in giving me a platform in which to write. The hearts and comments from hundreds of friends enabled me to endure the cancer experience and provided source material for this book.

Max Regan served as a wonderful developmental editor, muse, coach, and therapist.

Emi Clark sorted through my messy journals and lovingly photographed each picture of kindergarten art.

Trevor Clark provided valuable help in navigating the world of technology.

My Wednesday Writers' Group kept me on track as I wrote and edited stories one by one. Melanie Miller, Ellen Seaton, Diana Galindo, and Lana Hughes showed up consistently, helped me focus, and gave loving feedback.

The Boulder Writers' Retreat and especially Kim King provided a safe space for my first big, messy edit.

Chuck Johnson, Guida Jackson, Melanie Miller, Emi Clark, and Ellen Seaton read the rough manuscript and offered valuable suggestions for improvement. Melanie also did a terrific job of line editing, polishing the work, and clarifying concepts.

Mark Gelotte designed my cover and chapters and formatted my book for publication.

Lynette McGlamery lovingly proofread the book.

Forrest Clark was my greatest cheerleader.

These people are my village, my constant positive support. This book would not have happened without them.

Made in the USA
Coppell, TX
02 February 2020